Radiant

How to Have All the
Energy You Need
to Live a Life You Love

IRIS VAN OOYEN

EASTWOOD
PRESS

First edition. Published by Eastwood Press.
www.radiantbook.nl

Paperback ISBN: 978-90-828220-3-8
Hardcover ISBN: 978-90-828220-7-6
Ebook ISBN: 978-90-828220-5-2

Edited by Allison K Williams
Cover and interior design by Domini Dragoone
Cover and author photos by Heidi Hapanowicz

To all the sensitive souls
finding and carving their own path.

CONTENTS

Preface

Being tired and exhausted seems like a disease
of this time. I know some people wear it like a badge of honor—just
like being busy.

I believe it is *not* normal to be tired most of the time. It is a sign
of something wrong. A disbalance. In this book, I will help you
uncover the reasons why you may be tired and what you can do to
change that. I believe we all have access to an eternal well of energy;
even when you are physically ill, there is a lot of energy to be gained
by using your existing reserve more wisely.

> **TRUTH**: We must learn how to take good care of
> ourselves, because we have never been taught.

Lack of energy directly impacts your productivity, your ability
to be creative (hello problem solving!), and your capacity to be discerning. When you are tired, chances are you take things way more
personally than when you are balanced and rested. I will show you

1

how having more energy will not only increase your productivity and creativity—it will enhance your overall well-being. Life is too short to be miserable. It's time to start loving your life.

If you are reading this book, then somewhere deep down you know there is more energy available for you, too; no matter your age, your physical condition, or your profession.

I'm excited to embark on this journey together and dive deeper into the world of energy. Let's discover where you can find more energy so you can enjoy life more fully, and shine!

My Journey

I'm the girl who did everything the way I was expected to. The corporate job. The brand-new house. The handsome husband.

I was the "good" girl. And once I'd achieved everything I thought I'd ever wanted...I was the miserable girl.

Burnt out at the age of twenty-four.

A perfectionist who took on too much responsibility because I cared so much—about my demanding job, my family, and how other people felt in general.

I wanted everything to work out for everyone. In fact, I was so busy taking care of everybody else, I forgot to take care of myself. Instead of sitting down to relax I cleaned the house, visited my recently widowed mother-in-law and tried to be the perfect wife.

I had to take naps in the afternoon to be able to stay awake for dinner. I finally ended up at a naturopath who told me, "You have energy for four hours per day and you do the rest on willpower..."

Part of me was proud for sticking it out on pure will, until he finished his sentence.

"...and it is damaging your organs."

His words hit me like a brick. I felt like I had barely started my life and somehow I was already harming my organs. All my efforts to be a good girl had come at a steep cost.

After that I changed my life. I started a strict diet to rebalance my body, learned to relax, and went to international retreats and conferences.

When I started exploring what I truly wanted rather than what was expected from me, I came to understand I was a sensitive soul and understood how that impacted my energy level.

I learned to read my inner compass and sense my intuition, often getting chills of confirmation. And I realized I had access to a far more valuable tool than my mind alone.

I discovered the value of being true to myself—even when it was hard.

I said "No" to 50% of my business to free up time to develop my intuitive skills, left a marriage that was no longer fulfilling me, and rejected a million-dollar offer.

In truth it was never the easier path.

I cried a lot, said "No" a lot, learned to breathe through disappointing other people, and embraced who I am.

Good girls burn out. Powerful ones let go.

By delving into a world of self-care, seeking community, and investing in my personal development, I learned to look at challenges and grow from them. Learned to see my life as an opportunity in shifting perspective. To let go of judgment and meet others where they are.

Rather than force myself to pick one passion and be done with it, I followed an inner nudge. Allowed myself to pursue VARIETY.

I created an all-natural line of essential oil essences.

I wrote a novel. (In English—my second language.)

I tapped into my professional network to facilitate brainstorming sessions and teambuilding, and—my flagship service—I became a transformational mentor, helping people recover from their life of overdoing, overperforming, overgiving, and living beneath overcast skies. When what they really want is freedom to be themselves. To live in color. To love their life.

By widening my focus, I discovered I flourish when I'm doing multiple things. So when you want to remove the reins, stop wedging the vision for your life into a single idea, liberate yourself from the wave of external expectations…just know there is a way out.

The first half of my life I lived on willpower—Forceful. Obedient. Driven. Often blind. Sometimes destructive.

Remember the miserable girl?

Until I tapped into my SWEET POWER™— Curious. Trusting. Allowing. Often playful. Always envisioning.

Because we NEED power that cares for others and the world and gets things done. But that power is extremely finite if you don't know how to tap into its eternal source.

Let's be honest about how you spend your time and energy. Get clear on what you prioritize and where you are holding yourself prisoner. Because you can beat your head against the wall as much as you want but ultimately you are the one that has to change.

You hold all the power. All you have to do is access it.

Introduction

I think you can't (or shouldn't) write a book about energy management when you don't know what it's like to be tired and exhausted. It so happens I've had plenty of experience with that. None of it on purpose, obviously. But it has given me ample opportunity to learn—not only what it's like, but what you need in order to recharge, to refill that battery, and what to do differently the next time to avoid the same outcome. What is needed to not just get by, but to live life fully.

In this book I share parts of my personal journey, but more importantly I reveal the tips and insights that have helped me as a sensitive soul to move from being drained to having plenty of energy. The tools and techniques I learned and developed in the past thirty years have been tried first by me, and then applied by thousands of clients.

I believe this book contains the keys to support you, too, as you find a happy, healthy balance for your life and your body so that you have the energy and the time to savor it.

When we were born, none of us came with a manual, as annoying as that must have been for our parents and caretakers. I have often longed for a guidebook for myself.

I hope this book can be part of your manual for life—learning how to take good care of yourself and consciously manage your energy so you can thrive.

This book is for you if you're struggling with your energy level. When you often feel drained or exhausted, when you feel like your life is running you rather than having plenty of time and energy to enjoy life and the people around you, when you live from weekend to weekend or simply know you used to have more energy when you were younger. This is the perfect timing for you to stumble upon this book.

As I mentioned, I'm a sensitive soul. In fact, about 20% of the population is highly sensitive. You can take my free Sensitivity Quiz at **www.radianttools.nl** and discover within minutes whether you are a sensitive soul, too. If you are, there is an even bigger need for the tools in this book.

We have forgotten how to listen to our body and hear what it's telling us. We have drowned out or ignored its signals for so long, we no longer know what it's saying. That's what causes most of the physical problems and disbalance. I will help you get back in touch with your body to hear what it is trying to tell you, so you can act accordingly.

You are probably reading this book because what you are currently doing no longer supports you in managing your energy. What used to work no longer does the trick because you have changed. As you grow and develop, you become more sensitive and need different and more powerful tools to manage your energy and sensitivity. As you progress, it becomes more important to set healthy boundaries. Chances are, you can no longer get away with what you used to be able to get away with. Your soul is asking you to step it up and this is your chance to learn *how* to manage your energy and take back control. So you can go from being overwhelmed and exhausted to being grounded and centered and clear.

> **TRUTH**: Lack of energy is a symptom.
> It is not the original problem.

The first layer of your exhaustion might be a physical imbalance or the fact you are giving your energy away. What is underneath that first layer is the deeper reason you don't have enough energy. That underlying cause is the root problem.

When it comes to managing your energy there is often an underlying reason why you are not taking good care of yourself. The lack of self-care is the result of a fundamental problem. Over time, not having enough energy, focus, and happiness has become problematic. But when we dive into a deeper layer, we will see why this became a problem in the first place. If we were having this conversation one-on-one I would be able to sense what the root cause is for you. Given that this is a book, I will do my best to highlight the most common reasons so that you gain insight into which problem is prevalent for you. This will allow you to get clear on *why* you are slacking on your self-care. To understand why somehow, something has been holding you back from taking the utmost care of yourself.

Having said that, we will start by making sure you have more energy so you have the bandwidth to actually begin looking at the original, underlying problem.

Each section ends with an invitation to help you put the insights into practice.

You will receive an energetic upleveling while you take in this book. You may need some time to yourself to integrate the insights after each chapter. You may feel the need to take a nap in the coming days and when you have a headache drink extra water, because that means you are cleansing and letting go. And no, you are not doing anything wrong if this does not happen for you. These shifts impact each person differently.

I look forward to sharing my experiences and tools with you and I am so honored and excited you are here!

Enjoy the journey :)

CHAPTER 1

Discovering Sensitive Souls

I didn't know I was highly sensitive until my late twenties. I went to a workshop on creative thinking and one of the participants gave me her card. She told me to call her because she wanted to share something with me. I must have sensed that phone call would change my life because I put it off for three whole months.

Once we spoke, we stayed on the phone for three hours straight. She told me I was highly sensitive and it was time to actively start using my intuition. I had no idea what she was talking about because I was so used to relying on my thinking mind. Until she shared some examples. I totally recognized myself in her stories but I had never realized some of my experiences were unusual for most people. For instance, I thought everyone got home after shopping with a splitting headache. Everyone says shopping is tiring so I always figured we were talking about the same degree of being tired. It hadn't occurred to me, the level of tired could be different for some people. I'm grateful I ran into her when I did, because most people do not discover their sensitivity until much later.

I also realized there were many situations where my intuition had led me somewhere. Like visiting my maternal grandfather against all odds on a school night—simply because I felt the urge to go, despite everyone telling me to wait. He passed away the next morning.

Since that wakeup call, I have spent most of my time recognizing and developing my intuitive insights and honing my ability to bring through healing energy to get to the core of what people need.

What Is a Sensitive Soul?

A sensitive soul is someone who has a heightened awareness of EVERYTHING. Sensitivity is the ability to pick up on nuances and details not everyone notices. This has to do with how these people process stimuli in the brain and how they perceive other people's emotions and energy fields. Elaine N. Aron coined the term "highly sensitive" and her research shows how highly sensitive people have a more complex and detailed way of processing sensory input (Aron 2004). They sort stimuli in many more categories than other people.

Usually, a person has one specific sense that is most sensitive—for example, some people are extremely sensitive to sound or smells—but most FEEL too much. When you notice so many things, it is easy to get overwhelmed because you are continually overstimulated. Your senses are literally on overload because you are aware of everything going on around you. You hold on to more details than most people.

Highly sensitive people are often referred to as HSPs. I prefer the term "sensitive souls." Most sensitive souls live in a constant state of overwhelm—I know I did. Usually because they either don't know they are highly sensitive or they don't know how to manage their sensitivity. And that costs a lot of energy and can make you cranky or moody.

Characteristics of sensitive souls:

* You can sense people's emotions.
* Noise or the "wrong" kind of music drains you.
* You are easily distracted and find it hard to focus.

* You sometimes just "know" things.
* You can feel sad or angry for no apparent reason.
* You feel like there is something wrong with you, because not everybody is impacted by things the way you are.
* Sometimes you simply feel too much.
* When you have to do too many things at once you get irritated.
* You often feel misunderstood and alone.
* When you have been around other people you need time on your own to recharge.

These are some of the most apparent traits of sensitive souls, but the list is not complete. You can take my free Sensitivity Quiz to find out if you're a sensitive soul—though I'm guessing you are more sensitive than the average person, and that's why you are reading this. In my experience most—if not all—sensitive souls are highly intuitive as well.

When you don't consciously manage your sensitivity, chances are you experience some negative side effects of being sensitive. And you don't need to! We'll look at managing your sensitivity in Chapter 8.

However, you don't need to be a sensitive soul to benefit from the insights and practical tips in this book and to increase the amount of energy you have! In addition, the advice on being sensitive might help you understand and better support a sensitive friend or partner.

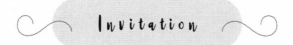

Invitation

If you have not already taken the Sensitivity Quiz I recommend you do so now, as it will be helpful to know moving forward. You can find the free quiz at **www.radianttools.nl.**

CHAPTER 2

Signs Revealing You Need to Manage Your Energy

I hung up the phone and sat back on the edge of the bed. My parents had just spent the better half of the conversation trying to convince me I had to be careful and slow down. Telling me I was doing too much. That I was treading in dangerous territory.

I disagreed. I was doing fine. Honestly, I was a little annoyed they kept nagging me. It wasn't the first time they had raised this topic.

Two weeks later, it turned out they were right.

While having tea with my dear friend (a nurse), she told me straight-up, "You're suffering from burnout."

I still wasn't convinced. She suggested I make a list of all the physical symptoms I was experiencing and that she would come back after half an hour. Turns out I filled an entire PAGE with things ranging from dizziness and headaches to being nauseous.

Confronting that list, I realized this was not normal. That something might be off after all.

The next morning, she took me to her doctor. Even though my partner and I had moved there a year before, I didn't have a physician yet. The doctor looked at my list, asked me some questions, and then confirmed my friend's verdict. He told me to call my boss and tell him I was suffering from burnout and had no idea how long this process would take. The doctor emphasized that last part. Then he told me to come back in two weeks.

To me, two weeks seemed like a very long time. So I asked, "What if I've recovered before then?"

He gave me a smile and the best answer he could've given me, "Then you come back sooner."

Somehow that eased my mind. Of course I didn't go back earlier. All in all, I stayed home for three months before slowly easing back into my (demanding) corporate marketing job as product manager for a well-known Dutch chocolate brand.

Looking back, it wasn't a matter of *if* I would run into that brick wall, but *when*.

My father-in-law had passed away a few months earlier and his loss had hit us all hard. Being the only in-law made me feel not just responsible for the well-being of my boyfriend at the time, but for his mother and brother as well. At work, my boss had been transferred and I was doing most of her work on top of my own. Being highly perfectionistic and having a huge sense of responsibility ensured I was pulling more than my weight there as well. Combined with a traffic-packed commute, playing house for the first time, and suffering from hypoglycemia I didn't discover until years later at my naturopath, it was disaster waiting to happen. And happen it did.

My burnout taught me a lot. I can't say I'm glad it happened, but I am grateful for the insights that intense period brought me and the changes it forced me to make in my life and the way I lived it.

If you haven't experienced a burnout you can't really understand what it's like. I got worse before I got better. When I stopped pushing through and no longer functioned on adrenaline, I started to feel how tired I truly was.

That same girlfriend who took me to her doctor helped me find a rhythm for my days at home. As chance would have it, she was on maternity leave and thankfully had the flexibility to keep an eye on me. And I am so very blessed she did. Equipped with her *own* experience of a severe burnout, she was the best support I could've hoped for.

One of the most vivid memories of that period is what I call "Asparagus Day." I went to the store armed with a shopping list: asparagus, ham, eggs, and a few other things. Stop one was the produce department. I searched high and low for asparagus. Turned out they were out of stock. Aha. A sane person would have taken that as a cue to grab another vegetable. Not burned-out me. No, I cheerily went on to collect ham and eggs. The perfect side dish to asparagus.

That night my boyfriend asked, "What's for dinner?"

I thought hard. "Asparagus!"

"Oh nice!" He headed for the kitchen and returned after several minutes. "I can't find any."

I thought longer and harder. "That's right! They were out of stock."

I'm sure you can imagine his bewildered look. We ate an omelet instead.

Now, I consider myself to be well-educated, smart, and wildly practical. This incident highlighted what bad shape I was in. If I hadn't been there myself, I would think someone had to be extremely dumb in order to pull this off. Apparently, burnout had affected my brain much more than I realized.

> **TRUTH**: When you're slowly burning out, you don't see it coming. You don't realize what's truly happening; it's such a gradual process. You get used to the changes in your body, the lowering of your energy, the sneaky increase in brain fog.

Using the tools in this book might help you catch things early on or alert you to the fact you are operating on adrenaline, not true energy. There is an entire chapter on pushing through. Also, if people warn you—it might be time to listen. I know that's one of the hardest parts because you literally can't see it until you do. Sometimes we have to hit the wall before our eyes are opened.

Exhaustion Impacts Your Entire Being

We all go through periods when we are more tired than usual, which we may consider normal. When you are not sleeping enough, for whatever reason, that will have a direct impact on your energy level and your productivity. Simply ask new parents, students cramming for their exams, or travelers with jet lag.

I remember when I worked at the centennial Olympic Games in Atlanta. It was a thrilling time and a unique experience, and I've never slept as little as I did in those weeks. The days were long and we had a forty-five-minute commute to the friends-of-a-friend's place where we rented a room (cockroaches included). Even though it was the middle of summer, we always left and arrived in the dark. The day after the closing ceremony I returned "home" on MARTA (the metro), and even though it was still afternoon, I was fighting to stay awake. My eyes kept closing and I feared I would miss my stop.

Valid reasons for being very tired are:
* Lack of sleep.
* A peak in work activity or continued stress.
* An illness, injury, surgery, etc.
* Emotional upheaval.
* Intense physical exercise.

There are different kinds of exhaustion. There is the physical exhaustion from not enough sleep, like during my Olympic Games.

There is the physically ill, "I can't even lift my hand I'm so drained" exhaustion. Like the moment my brother and dad had to carry me up the stairs like a sack of potatoes after an unfortunate fall on my head. The utter exhaustion from the aftermath of the fall had rendered me unable to move.

There is the emotionally exhausted. I remember the first weeks and months after my divorce: not only were there a million practical things to take care of, but it was emotionally taxing to find a new balance after letting go of my partner of thirteen years. Emotions eat energy like nothing else. As a result I lost a lot of weight I did not have the luxury of losing.

Asparagus Day is a great example of being mentally exhausted.

The seasons impact us as well. That's why I dedicated Chapter 21 to this. In the winter when there is less sunlight, our bodies literally have less energy.

I know from experience what it's like to have very little energy, due to physical problems or working too hard, and also because I am highly sensitive. I've had years where I needed to take a nap in the afternoon to get through the day, or struggled to stay awake to actually eat dinner. So I learned to recognize the signs of when you need to start managing your energy to avoid it leaking away.

The real question is whether your lack of energy is due to something temporary that is "normal" and logical, or whether something is off that needs your attention. Like an oncoming burnout or other imbalances in your body.

It is important to be aware that your lack of energy will not only show up in your physical body as feeling tired—which is the clearest, most obvious sign you are low on energy—but it will also show up mentally, emotionally, and energetically.

These lists are not conclusive but they give you an idea of which problems a lack of energy can cause.

Physical signs: often, our body tells us
we are running out of energy.

* ✳ When you wake up you feel sluggish, as if you are wading through mud.
* ✳ You regularly catch a cold and it takes a long time for it to go away.
* ✳ You feel like you are always tired and forever catching up.
* ✳ At the end of the day or week you often experience a headache.
* ✳ There are moments when you suddenly feel drained, as if someone removed your battery.
* ✳ You always get ill on vacation.
* ✳ You have to take sick days more than twice a year (a clear indication your body is struggling).

Mental signs: when you are low on energy it
impacts the workings of your mind, as well.

* ✳ You find it hard to stay focused and to concentrate.
* ✳ You are forgetting things or experiencing short-term memory dysfunction.
* ✳ You have "mind-fog" that slows you down.
* ✳ You do not get as much work done as you used to.
* ✳ You have difficulty coming up with certain words or you blurt out the wrong word (not what you were trying to say).
* ✳ Your to-do list feels endless and more demanding than what you have energy (or time) for.
* ✳ Your thoughts are going a mile a minute.
* ✳ You are not as creative as you normally are.
* ✳ You have trouble falling asleep because you keep thinking about all the things you still need to do or should have done differently.

Emotional signs: being tired often
causes more volatile emotions.

* You experience mood swings and can get angry for no
  apparent reason.
* You are unhappy.
* You are easily irritated.
* You feel unbalanced, sometimes even out of control.
* You cry more easily than usual.
* You feel overwhelmed.
* You sometimes know you are being unreasonable but you
  can't seem to help yourself (and afterwards you feel bad for
  being such a b*tch).
* It feels like there is no solution in sight.

Signs of energetic problems: when you are
drained, it is easier to stay stuck in your head
and forget all about your energetic system.

* You find it more difficult than usual to get grounded
  and centered.
* After working with a client or meeting with someone,
  you are tired.
* You feel spacey and out of sorts.
* It is hard not to be affected by other people's moods.
* Your energy feels heavy.

As you can see, not having enough energy impacts your entire
system. Which makes sense because when you do not have enough
gas in the tank, none of the parts get the fuel they need to function properly.

If any of these signs sound familiar, it means you are losing
energy you do not need to lose. These signs also mean you are putting a strain on your physical body. Which is acceptable for a short

period, but if you put too much stress on your body for too long, you might end up with chronic problems.

If you recognize more than five signs in total on these lists, consider this your wake-up call. It is time to start listening to your body and rearrange your priorities. Your health demands it.

The good news is our body tells us what it needs and when it's overburdened. We only need to (re)learn how to listen—and then act accordingly.

Telltale Signs From Your Body

We all have a "weak" spot in our body. I'm sure you know what yours is. We all have a telltale physical sign that signals to us that we are off-balance and pushing too hard; that our body needs rest. Whether it is your tummy or a headache, stiffness in your lower back or a sore throat—it is usually the same part of your body that caves first.

Whenever your signal spot acts up, you must take a break and pause. Take inventory and decide what you can do *now* to return to better balance.

Let me ask you: how often do you stop and listen; how often do you rearrange your schedule when your signal spot is asking for your attention? I know when we *do* listen, we deplete our body less and our recovery time is much quicker. Same as when you have a common cold. When you take the time to rest and heal you will be fit in perhaps even a day. If you push through, take an aspirin or plainly ignore the cold and keep working, you lower the vitality in your body.

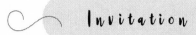

Invitation

Write down what your signal spot is. The next time it alerts you, I invite you to take immediate action and lower your load. This is your body asking for your attention. The sooner you respond, the faster you will return to balance (and the less you will damage yourself!).

CHAPTER 3

The Foundation: Grounding

Start by being aware of your body. Our body speaks to us all the time, except most of us have forgotten how to listen because we are too busy being in our heads. In order to get back in touch with your body and hear what it's saying to you, you must be grounded.

Grounding saved my life—or at least my sanity—one day when I was in New York City to attend meetings. That Sunday I was hosting a workshop right off Fifth Avenue. I was looking forward to tuning in for participants and helping them get clear on what was holding them back. I enjoy supporting people in embracing more of who they truly are. But it wasn't your regular weekend. I stayed at a friend's fourteenth-floor apartment. I was there by myself, and Saturday night the howling winds kept me awake. When I *felt* the wind on my face while lying in bed, I got nervous and switched on the light. That's when I saw the glass of the window bulging inward. There was water on the floor, leaking through the windowpanes. Hurricane Sandy was on her way.

Sunday morning the city announced the closing of the subways, so I quickly packed all my luggage. The concierge told me to order a town car as hailing a cab would be near impossible. No point staying in Harlem when both my workshop and meetings were downtown. I arrived at the workshop location a little frenzied, but on time to do my regular preparation, including getting myself centered and grounded by using my signature grounding exercise (which I'll teach you later in this chapter). That's when the first cancellations came in. Participants didn't want to risk coming over, or they were simply leaving town. My Monday meeting was canceled because the city ordered all buildings over a certain number of stories closed.

I had thirty minutes to spare before the workshop started and I used that time to change (and print!) my ticket and secure a seat on the last plane out of NYC to Europe. I would need to change planes in Paris, but I was thrilled to be able to get out before the hurricane hit full force the next day. Through some miracle I was able to get another town car to take me to the airport right after the workshop. I made it to the gate with minutes to spare AND I gave a really good workshop.

The only reason I was able to do all that was because I was centered and grounded, which allowed me to focus and concentrate on what needed to be done and in which order. The normal human instinct might have been to panic, or rush around to get more info. If I had panicked, I would have had to find shelter during the hurricane. Instead, I deliberately slowed down and focused on one thing at a time.

What Is Grounding?

When you spend a lot of time behind a computer, in meetings, or talking on the phone, a lot of your energy goes to your head. When you are fully centered and grounded, your energy is spread evenly throughout your physical body. When you are not, a disproportionate amount of energy is present above your shoulders.

Let's say your head is 10% of the size of your physical body. In order for the energy to be spread evenly, your brain is entitled to 10% of your energy, maybe a little more. Of course your brain needs a lot of power to function, but I am referring to your energetic energy.

The average person will have 70% of their energy present in their head, leaving only 30% for the rest of their body. This makes most people top-heavy. When you are "in your head," you will notice it is hard to shut down your thoughts. Likely you only use the upper half of your chest when breathing.

Take a moment to see where your breath is focused right now. Place a hand on your lower belly and one on your upper chest. Which hand moves the most when you inhale and exhale?

> **TIP:** Ideally only your lower hand moves. Grounding will help you lower and deepen your breathing.

These are signs you are not fully grounded:

* ✶ Your breathing is high (chest instead of belly).
* ✶ You often have cold feet.
* ✶ You have trouble falling asleep.
* ✶ Your thoughts go a mile a minute.
* ✶ Difficulty to focus and concentrate.
* ✶ Your energy is all over the place.
* ✶ You are often tired.
* ✶ You are always busy and cannot seem to find time to relax.
* ✶ You feel scattered.
* ✶ It is hard for you to sit down and do nothing.
* ✶ You feel you are not in control; you do not have a grip on yourself.
* ✶ You have difficulty hearing your intuition.

If any of this sounds familiar then it means you are not spreading the energy evenly throughout your body. Grounding is the first thing I teach all my private clients. It is the number one foundational practice and the key to energy management.

> **TRUTH**: Most people do not center themselves thoroughly enough or often enough.

Grounding is not something you can do once and be done with. It requires permanent attention. You cannot shower on Monday for the rest of the week, either. Or drink lots of water today and not need any tomorrow. Grounding has to become a daily practice. I recommend you start by grounding in the morning and every evening.

When you want to take good care of yourself and grow and evolve, this is where it starts. Grounding is the basis on which you build a healthy life full of energy, so make sure you know how to ground before moving on to something else.

I have seen many times where people think they already know how to ground, or believe they don't need to do it, or trust because they take a walk outside that that's enough. And it's not. You might be the rare exception, but unless you walk around feeling powerfully rooted to the point where it feels like you couldn't tip over even if you wanted to, you are not grounded to your maximum depth.

If you struggle to hold someone's attention you are probably not grounded. When people are not connecting with you but are looking away or up—they're in their head. When you are fully present, you command attention in a positive way. A present person is usually a very attractive person in the most literal sense of the word.

Meditation is not the same as grounding. Some forms of meditation might help you ground, but, in general I recommend grounding yourself *before* you start meditating. If you center yourself first, it will be easier to stay focused on your meditation. See grounding as a shortcut with immediate results, whereas meditation might help you get rooted as a side effect. There is more than one way to ground. I will highlight the two that my clients have found the most helpful.

> **TIP:** Standing when you are grounding makes it easier and more powerful. Especially when you are still learning to ground fully.

> ∽ EXERCISE ∽
>
> Stand. Place your feet flat on the floor. Lean forward, shifting your weight to the front as much as you can while keeping the entire soles of your feet flat on the floor. Now do the same leaning backward, then sideways, left, and right. Repeat this cycle at least five times.

This exercise shifts your focus to your feet and out of your head. It helps bring your energy down from your brain into the rest of your body so it is more evenly spread, like it is supposed to be.

Do not worry if you did not feel any difference. It took me weeks to feel a change and get out of my head and into my body. I stood next to my bed countless times, wobbling on my feet, wondering whether I was doing it right. Grounding did not come naturally to me. They often say you are here to teach what you have learned, and that certainly applies in this case. I hope by sharing my specific process, you'll find grounding easier than I did.

Steps to ground with ease:

* ✻ Stand when you ground.
* ✻ Take off high heels.
* ✻ Make sure your feet rest flat on the floor.
* ✻ Place a hand on your lower belly to help deepen your breathing.
* ✻ Straighten your spine.
* ✻ Use the same location: I noticed this creates an energetic vortex and will help you ground faster once you have done this exercise several times.

I discovered that last one by accident. I always stood in the middle of my office in order to ground before a client call. One day there was a box in that exact spot so I stood next to the box. Somehow it did not feel right. I ended up moving the box so I could stand in "my" spot. To my surprise, I immediately felt the difference. Thanks to that box I realized I had created what I now call a "grounding vortex."

I also noticed it's harder to stay grounded when I wear high heels, synthetic clothing, or pantyhose. If you have difficulty grounding and you have an important meeting or performance, then I recommend wearing flat shoes and cotton socks or go barefoot if that's appropriate.

In order to make grounding part of your routine, pick a moment in the day that works for you. I ground after brushing my teeth (which covers the beginning and end of the day), and before every client session or workshop. To start with, you can hang a sticky note on your bathroom mirror (or whichever location works for you) to remind yourself to ground and help ingrain this habit.

Pay extra attention to grounding when you work a lot on the computer or with your mind. Whenever you feel your thoughts drifting, it pays to take a moment to center yourself.

You can find the complimentary audio recording for this Quick Grounding Activation at **www.radianttools.nl**. This audio will more easily guide you through my signature grounding exercise, but if you prefer you can read a short version of this grounding activation here instead:

Place both feet firmly on the floor.

Feel the weight of your feet resting on the floor.

Give yourself permission to be fully present in this moment.

Place a hand on your lower belly to invite your breathing to deepen. With every exhale, send your energy and your awareness to your feet and the earth beneath you.

Breathe at your own pace. Feel how with every breath out you become more aware of your physical body.

Let any excess energy in your head slowly trickle down, spreading itself evenly throughout your physical body. Trusting that the energy knows where to go.

Return your focus to your feet. Feel how they're resting on the floor. Imagine that from the soles of your feet, roots are growing into the earth—just as if you were a tree. Let these roots grow downwards, sideways, creating a vast network of roots allowing you to be more centered and grounded.

Continue to expand these roots as long as you like (ideally until you sense a difference). Feel how your feet become heavier and heavier.

Then take a deep breath in, and on your exhale release any tension you're still holding in your body.

Slowly come back to the present. Wiggle your fingers and toes, and when you're ready, open your eyes.

I personally prefer this exercise over the wobbling feet because it takes me much deeper, much faster. Your experience might be different. Again, listening to the audio and allowing yourself to be guided, without having to lead your own exercise while doing it, can be more effective than trying to do this from the book.

How can you tell you are more grounded than you were before the exercise?

* A heaviness in your feet or legs.
* A sense that your energy or weight is more evenly distributed throughout your body.
* You have more contact with the ground, standing more firmly on the floor.
* Your mind has calmed down, with fewer thoughts running around your head.
* Tingling in your feet or legs.

Don't stop because you did not yet feel a difference. The good news is that the more often you do this, the easier and faster it becomes. It's like a muscle that needs training. The more you exercise grounding yourself, the "deeper" that centering becomes and the longer it lasts.

People often forget to take care of their physical body and think they only need their mind to do their job well. If you ignore what your body needs, you will get sick and then you will not be able to work. Or at least not as well.

When you are grounded you might recognize a loss of energy or disbalance in the early stage. Allow yourself to course-correct by taking a break or going to bed early. This will prevent problems from adding up to the point where you need a lot of effort to recharge your battery because you have depleted yourself completely.

If at this point you're thinking, *that sounds nice but I'm kinda reading this book because I let stuff add up,* then no worries! That's what I am here to help you with.

> T I P: In order to tap into your intuition,
> you need to be grounded.

When you start to ground, you become more aware of your physical body. Chances are you will become conscious of how tired you truly are. You already were this exhausted, but you were simply unaware of it because you were not fully present in your body. Please do not think you can fix it by grounding less. That's like pretending there is no dirty laundry as long as you keep the hamper closed. Tempting, I know. But you will still have to deal with it at some point. Better sooner than later, because it will only become more difficult the longer you put it off.

"Woo-woo people" are usually not grounded. To me, woo-woo indicates people who are engrossed in their spirituality to the point where it feels unbalanced. They are often overly focused on the spiritual aspects of life. In Dutch, the word for woo-woo is *zweverig,* "floating," and I like how that indicates the lack of being rooted.

I've seen instances where people were so excited about being able to connect to higher wisdom that they stopped taking good care of their physical body. As you build and expand your intuition you need to build and expand your ability to ground as well. You need to have a larger anchor if the ship gets bigger! I believe it's dangerous to open up to intuitive insights when you're not grounded, because you will no longer be able to be discerning. Your discernment helps you see whether you're listening to your fear or to your intuition.

Spiritually aware people sometimes forget that you have to live life here, in the physical realm. And you can only do that, and use and support your physical body, when you are grounded. That is how you can make an impact.

Additional Grounding Support

There are different ways to support your body in being grounded. In addition to the specific grounding exercises, you can take a walk in the woods. Walking is better than running. You may enjoy working in the garden. Being in nature is very centering, especially if you get to touch the soil or the trees.

Use essential oils to ground yourself. Massage a drop of pure lavender oil on both your temples. Diffusing cedarwood or pine tree oil also helps you center, bringing a lovely scent into your home in the process.

Foods that help you ground are extra-dark chocolate, beet root, ginger, and many other foods that grow underground. Think root vegetables. Make sure you eat enough solid foods too, since salads on their own will not help you ground. Participants of my in-person workshops know it's my tradition to gift each participant their own organic dark chocolate bar. A powerful and enjoyable way to stay grounded as we dive in deep.

To top things off, perhaps enjoy a bath with Himalayan salt or Dead Sea salt. This helps cleanse your energy field as well. A great excuse to take a bath! You can tell your partner it's homework. As an alternative, you could use Epsom salt. I personally feel Himalayan salt works best and is the most gentle while being very effective. You can take a salt foot bath if you have no access to a full bath or if it's too warm, given the season.

Being grounded is one thing. Staying grounded through stress, busyness, changing schedules, and physical challenges is the real deal. That's what will give you a leading edge. You will not be as affected by what is going on around you. You will be able to use your power—not your force—to make your way through. Staying grounded is really basic, but can be challenging at the same time.

Last week, when my dad called to tell me my mother had been rushed to the hospital and was undergoing emergency surgery, it came as a complete shock. To make matters worse, I had to give an online training for twenty people an hour later. I called a dear friend, had a good cry to get the stress out of my system, and then made sure I was thoroughly grounded and calm, ready to focus on my training.

The more you practice grounding, the more you strengthen your ability to concentrate on one single thing, unbothered by what else is going on around you or in your life. So you can give your full focus and energy to that one thing, being most productive and efficient.

The simple tool of grounding has made a big difference in my life. But it needs practice! Keep at it until you can feel a shift. It might take time, but I know you, too, have the ability to ground.

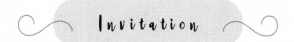

Invitation

Experiment with the wobbling feet and Quick Grounding Activation audio at **www.radianttools.nl** and see what works best for you. Start by making grounding part of your routine so you will not forget it. For me, I prefer to ground after brushing my teeth. Find your own moment to anchor this into daily activities. Make sure you ground at least each morning and each evening. It will help get you ready for the day and sleep better, and often deeper, at night.

Play with the other ways to ground as well, but see those as additional tools. Walking in the woods and eating chocolate are just extra. I recommend you use the "official" exercises to stand up and ground.

CHAPTER 4

Measuring Your Energy

Actively managing your energy is important, especially when you do not appear to have enough. I know it is not something everyone thinks about consciously. You either have energy or you are tired. By learning how to manage your energy, you will discover you can have more of it. Plus you can make the limited supply of energy you do have last longer.

When you have enough energy you are more productive and creative. You will feel happier and healthier. The list of benefits goes on and on.

How Much Energy Do You Think You Have?

As a first step in getting a grip on managing your energy, we will get clear on how much energy you actually have and how it fluctuates throughout the day. Because in order to be able to manage your energy you must know what drains and what recharges you. I developed a powerful tool for this: the Daily Energy Inventory. This helps you monitor your energy and its fluctuations, and recognize the impact specific events and people have on you.

How to carry out an Energy Inventory:

* Each morning when you get up, take a moment to feel how much energy you have. This may seem funny, but some people wake up with less energy than they go to bed with.

* Give yourself a moment to get a sense of your body. Take inventory and pick a number between 0 and 100 to see where your energy level is at, and write that down using the tool below. If needed, you can use a number below zero. Just use your intuition to "feel" which number is appropriate. You can download the Daily Energy Inventory at **www.radianttools.nl** to fill in the form, or print it out.

* Check in again at the end of the day and write that number on the list, too.

* Do the same before and after you meet with a client or a friend (whether on the phone or in person), or go somewhere (supermarket, meeting, lunch, party, walk in the forest, etc.). This will help you get clear on what happens to your energy. Does it go up or down or does it stay the same?

* As an extra activity you can also track whether you are grounded.

* Take note of special situations or things that stand out and write that in the comments section.

Try not to judge yourself when you notice something costs you energy; instead, see it as a way of gathering data you can use to make changes.

Daily Energy Inventory

DATE: _____

ACTIVITY	BEFORE			AFTER			COMMENTS
	Current Time	Energy level 0–100	Grounded? YES / NO	Current Time	Energy level 0–100	Grounded? YES / NO	
Daily Check-In (morning and evening)							

Many people are not aware how much energy they leak during the day or what costs them energy. This simple but effective system helps you gain clarity. I highly suggest you do this, even if you think you already know what costs you the most energy. I know from experience there may be some surprises in there.

I recommend filling in the Daily Energy Inventory for at least a week. After you have done this for several days you can probably recognize patterns in the things that cost you energy, and it's highly important to be aware of that. The next step is ensuring you can change that, so you can have more energy.

> **TIP**: Be aware of false energy.

When you are stuck in overdrive it feels like you have plenty of energy to keep going. When you do a quick check-in you might think there is enough gas in the tank. If you truly listen to your body you will know when you are operating on adrenaline—which is what I call false energy—or whether you actually have sustainable energy left. Of course, all this is easier to sense when you are thoroughly grounded.

Right up until the moment I was made aware I was suffering from a burnout, I thought I was doing fine. I still got lots done; I didn't have a problem, *right?* One of the ways to recognize overdrive is that you are in your head. You feel like staying active and want to keep going. You tend to watch TV during your time off rather than read a book, meditate, or take a walk. These last three activities will help slow you down rather than continue to stimulate adrenaline production, and will make it easier to be in touch with your body.

I believe you know deep down that if you do not keep feeding the adrenaline you will "crash." Becoming conscious of your behavior and energy is essential, so you can make smart choices rather than push through.

If I could teach my younger self one thing, it would be how to manage my energy. It would have saved me a lot of time and frustration, and several health challenges, too. Even if it seems like you do not have the time (or the energy) to fill in this chart I urge you to do so, because it can be life-changing. You need more energy and this is the fastest way to clarity.

It pays to know which activities and people drain you the most, so you can be smart about what you do and who you see in the same day. Then you can try to balance your day and week with things that recharge you.

Just because you enjoy something does not necessarily mean it brings you energy. Most people think fun equals energy. Something might feel good in the moment, but it's very possible that the same activity drains you physically, energetically, or emotionally. That doesn't mean you shouldn't do it anymore, but this knowledge helps you be smart about when you do it and how often.

Another benefit of the Daily Energy Inventory is that this tool will alert you when you reach the crucial 20% threshold!

> **TRUTH**: You need 20% of your physical energy in order for your body to regenerate and recharge your battery back up to 100%.

What that means is your physical body needs 20% of its normal energy level to go through all the processes it executes at night (cell regeneration, digestion, and so on), so that you can end up with 100% of your energy in the morning.

Ideally, you stop your activities when your energy level dwindles to 20%. Doing so ensures you start the next day with a full tank. In practice, very few people do that. Most of us stop when we get tired (and often not even then).

When you are tired your energy is around 0-5%. Much too little for your body to recharge your battery to full capacity. Which means you will wake up in the morning with, let's say, 90% instead of 100%. The next day you sail past that sacred 20% level again (probably because you had no idea it was smart to stop there) and you push through until either you're tired or it's the end of the day. The following day you don't wake up with 90%, but maybe 85%.

If you do this over a longer period of time, it becomes quite clear why you might be tired often or why it feels like you used to have much more energy when you were younger. You have systematically depleted yourself.

It's not just your phone battery that needs to be recharged fully. Your body wants the same courtesy.

I know it's not easy to stop when you still have energy to do things—especially when you are bursting with ideas or have a large to-do list. But I have learned the hard way that it's the only smart thing to do. In the end it will save you time even though it feels counterintuitive.

Learning where your 20% lies will take a while, and you will overshoot the mark at first. And that's okay. It's part of the learning curve. I know it was one of the hardest things for me to learn. But you can only find that level if you start looking for it. Try to see it as an exploration in which you get to know yourself better, and remember not to beat yourself up when you have trouble finding your 20% gauge.

A friend of mine was working on an important deadline, but she was unwell. However, the deadline was of such importance she decided to push through. The problem was that after working for twenty minutes she needed to take a nap. I recommended she stop after fifteen minutes so she would not empty her tank entirely. She did and she got much more done, no longer needing that nap every time. Things like this seem counterintuitive, especially when you have so much to do. But it works to stop before you think you should, because you will recharge much faster.

Once you know what impacts your energy, it's important to try to find a balance between activities that give you energy and those that cost you energy, as you are still struggling to find a healthy balance and learning to increase the amount that you have. Be strict about what you choose to spend your time and energy on. The more you can give yourself the space to adhere to the 20% rule, the faster you will recharge your batteries and recover.

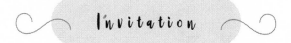

Invitation

Print the Daily Energy Inventory and use it consistently for at least one week. You can find it at **www.radianttools.nl.**

If you want to shift your current energy level, it means you have to start doing things differently. Most likely it does not mean doing more. Chances are it means doing less. Or at least doing less of what drains you, and more of what lights you up. It's time to let go of the "shoulds," as we'll cover in this book. You'll be required to make conscious decisions about where and how you use your time and energy and how you spend that energetic currency you have available.

If you want to take this a step further, you can monitor your resting heart rate when you wake up. Once you know what your baseline is you will notice when it goes up. This can be an early indication of a virus or infection. For elite athletes it can point toward getting overtrained. An increase in your resting heart rate might indicate an oncoming burnout as well.

Each of the following chapters will give you an idea of where you can gain energy and where you can stop giving it away or losing it. All these bits and pieces add up and before you know it, you have more energy than you have had in a long time. Enjoy the ride!

CHAPTER 5

Hidden Energy Drains

There are many things that can deplete you. You will discover several personal drains via your Energy Inventory, but I will share a few common ones here. Some of these drains can be so subtle they are hard to catch.

If you are highly sensitive, you will have even more elements that will cost you energy. If you have not yet taken the free quiz, now is a great time to do that. You can take the Sensitivity Quiz here: **www. radianttools.nl**. Within a few minutes you will know where you stand on the sensitivity scale.

As a sensitive soul I tend to notice all the little things that cost me energy. I've compiled everything I detected over the years in the following list.

Dehydration

Most people do not drink enough (good quality) water. Often our signal for thirst has weakened to the point we mistake it for hunger, so we eat something instead. Lack of water directly impacts our energy level and our ability to focus.

"A mere 2 percent drop in body water can trigger fuzzy, short-term memory trouble with basic math problems and result in difficulty focusing on the computer screen or printed page."
—Andreas Moritz, 2009

An adult needs at least six to eight large glasses of water per day. Be sure to steer clear from water that includes chlorine. Depending on where you live, the tap water might be good enough to drink. I'm fortunate with the quality of water in the Netherlands, but I still filter it. I can sense the difference—it makes the water softer and removes traces of heavy metals. If your home has copper pipes, you may want to have the quality of your water checked. Of course there are many good quality mineral waters available as well, but the downside is all the packaging.

Please know that coffee, black tea, soda, and alcohol are diuretics. Only water, herbal tea, and fresh juices are hydrating. When you drink a lot of coffee, you will need more water to compensate for the loss in fluids. (When you don't drink enough water you need to gradually increase your water intake to avoid health problems.)

Ionized water is a good way to support your body in eliminating pollutants. The negative ions generated in the water bind to the positively charged ions present in toxins. You can easily ionize water by boiling it for fifteen to twenty minutes. Take one or two sips per half hour. Keep the water warm in a thermos because it loses its power when it cools off (Moritz 1998 edition).

Temperature

Temperature of Your Environment
When a room is too warm or too cold, it costs your body energy to regulate your inner thermostat. Totally logical. You can diminish

the energy loss by dressing appropriately, turning down the heater, or shutting off the air-conditioning.

Temperature of Food and Drinks

Your body only processes food and drinks that are body temperature. Meaning when you drink something straight out of the fridge, your body will warm the liquid up to around 37 degrees Celsius (98.6 Fahrenheit) first—which costs precious energy.

For me, it was a revelation when I first learned about this. I was not aware that my body did not process anything when it was too cold, but it did explain why I preferred my beverages warmer. I simply did not have the energy to waste on heating liquids.

Food

Aside from the temperature of nutrition, the quality of what you feed yourself will make a big difference as well. When you eat organic food, your body does not have to dispel any toxins. The more whole foods you eat, the more nutrients your body gets.

In short: eat organic as much as you can. As a general rule, focus on the more fragile products first, if you have to make a choice about which organic produce to buy. The more fragile, the more pesticides a product usually includes. Think of berries, leafy greens, nectarines, and the like.

Do not put food in the microwave because there will be no nutrients left after you "nuke" your food. A microwave causes water molecules to vibrate so they heat the food, but in the process destroys vitamins, minerals, and the food's life force. This makes it harder to digest as well (Moritz 2009).

Avoid refined sugar and diet products (for example, products with aspartame). You might want to look into eating gluten-free. I made the change to eating gluten-free over two years ago and I'm so glad I did. A friend mentioned it would help minimize cramps when menstruating. For me, it worked wonders. I would say the pain level went down from fourteen to six (on a scale of ten). I basically gained two productive days per month. A word of caution: when you start eating gluten-free, it appears your body becomes less forgiving when you do eat gluten. Which makes sense. To me it's totally worth the trade-off, but I wish someone had warned me about that so I could have made that choice consciously. (You are welcome.)

When I was nineteen, I was diagnosed with mononucleosis. When I came home after class I had to take a nap before I could do anything else. This disease knocks most people out for a month. My version was less intense at the start (just one day of flu), but I was exhausted for months after. It was clear something needed to be done. I heard about a dietician who had helped someone else suffering from mono, and I visited her with the express intention of getting more energy from my food. She taught me a lot about different food combinations and supporting your body and its digestion. Applying her tips in combination with taking several supplements helped me gain some much-needed energy. Enough for me to graduate the next year and move to North Carolina where I did my MBA (and a list of extracurricular activities that makes me exhausted when I think back to it).

I'll never forget when the dietitian told me to steer clear of margarine. "When you take out certain ingredients, you need to replace them with others to keep it edible, spreadable, etc. More often than not, those new ingredients do more damage than the original ones." She recommended real butter. I couldn't be happier! I love butter. I've enjoyed organic butter since.

Skincare

The products you use on your skin can have a great impact on your energy and well-being. A significant part of what you put on your skin ends up in your bloodstream.

According to this article from the website *School of Public Health at Harvard*, "In the United States, the average person is exposed to more than a hundred chemicals from cosmetics, soaps, and other personal care products before leaving the house in the morning" (Roeder 2014).

Another Harvard article indicates that common chemicals in cosmetics interfere with hormones and can damage the nervous and immune system and may cause "unknown internal harm."

Steer clear from skincare, cosmetics, and hair products containing paraben or sodium laurel sulfate (SLS) and choose deodorant without aluminum. I have used all-natural and organic products for the past twenty years and clearly feel the difference. Your body can eliminate heavy metals and toxins ingested from beauty products or foods to a certain extent, but not, I believe, at the rate most people are exposed to. Better not to use your precious energy detoxing your body, when you can easily avoid harmful substances.

Physical Environment

Smell. Unpleasant smells can subtly drain your energy. Especially when it is one of your more dominant senses, like it is for me.

Light. Neither harsh nor too dim, as that strains your eyes, which—you got it—costs energy.

Amount of oxygen. Air your rooms daily (unless outside air quality is abominable).

Drafts. Air flow in a room can be distracting (I know it is to me), and it puts an extra strain on your body which can lead to stiff muscles and increases the risk of catching a cold.

Humidity. Dry air (<30% humidity) is linked to several respiratory tract issues, as well as irritated mucous membranes and dry skin. A healthy humidity level ranges between 40% and 60%. Dry air irritates the eyes as well.

Your chair and the height of your desk and screen. Make sure to check ergonomic standards so your posture is optimal when sitting.

(White) noise. Some people are super sensitive to sounds. A loud noise that might startle you will physically hurt them. Other noises that are present in the background might not be physically painful, but they will drain you. Tuning out background noise takes some of your energy, which is why noise-canceling headphones are popular. Most people prefer to do their thinking work in a quiet space for a reason. Not only are there fewer interruptions, but all your focus can go to the problem at hand. It takes about fifteen minutes to get into the flow. Each time you are interrupted, you have to start over again and get back into the zone. Quickly checking that text message costs much more time than the glance on your phone—you literally stopped the flow and have to crank things up again. Interruptions waste precious time and energy!

When I talk about "being in the flow," I'm referring to a state in which things seem to move without effort and you feel like you're on the right track. Actions and ideas fall into place and there's a perfect timing and synchronicity to everything that happens in your life. When you are not in the flow, things take more time and cost more energy—it may feel as if you're swimming upstream. In the flow, you'll likely feel calm and at ease, perhaps excited at how well things are going. Out of the flow you'll probably feel frustrated, like you can't find the right buttons to push to get things moving.

Impact of cell phones. Cell phone radiation and electromagnetic fields are all around us. A lot of people carry cell phones in their pockets. The good news is that you can do something to minimize the impact. For years I had a small, regular cell phone. I liked it and used it until it was completely worn out. Using it didn't particularly bother me, although I would notice a tingling in my hand when I was on longer calls. Then I decided to get a smartphone, mainly because that would allow me to check emails when abroad. I loved it. But after the first week, I was sitting on the couch wondering why I was so extremely tired. I went over the week in my head and there was no logical reason for my exhaustion. It was a regular week, nothing different than the one before. Until it hit me. The only difference was my phone. I had already heard that some smartphones seemed to have a stronger electromagnetic field than other phones but had not really given it a lot of thought. So I figured I better get one of those things that neutralized the radiation and see if that made a difference. It did. Big time. I'm now using it for my laptop as well. You can also place a large amethyst on your desk to counteract part of the electromagnetic radiation from your computer.

Synthetic clothing or synthetic duvet. They make it tougher to regulate your temperature. With natural materials your body can breathe more easily.

High heels. Heels make it more difficult to be grounded and in touch with your body, especially when wearing synthetic stockings.

Location

I've seen the impact of different locations firsthand, in my early work while facilitating brainstorming sessions and team-building activities, and in the last decade while leading workshops and retreats. A balanced room, that supports people's well-being, makes a huge difference in the energy level and also the effectivity and results of the event. I've seen spaces that drain people in no time—grey walls, fluorescent lighting, tiny windows and a view of the parking lot. That doesn't mean you can't get anything useful done, but it costs so much more effort and energy and it rarely feels easy and in the flow. When a space hits all the right spots, it's a joy to be there. People feel lighter and more supported. I dare say they even feel more joyful. As a result, sessions are so much more effective and creative.

I feel the difference in myself at the end of the day as well. In certain spaces I know I'll be utterly exhausted by the time we're done. Now if that surprises you, please keep in mind that these tools will not make you immune to energy loss. Remember the difference between being zapped by a draining environment or being tired because you worked out or worked hard. The latter are normal reasons for losing or using energy. It's about uncovering the sneaky energy drains that you don't need to suffer from, so you can consciously manage your energy and decide what you will use it for.

The more sensitive you are, the more subtle changes or shifts in some of these elements will impact you. The amount of energy lost with each item mentioned above might be small, but when your body does not have the luxury of abundant energy, all the little bits add up. Together they can make a big difference in how you feel and perhaps land you on the right side of the 20% threshold.

The hidden energy drains mentioned in this list are the more tangible ones. The more invisible drains will be covered in the rest of this book. Like taking on other people's energy and emotions or giving your energy away to other people.

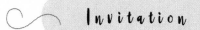

Invitation

Which drains stood out most? Pick one or two that you can (start to) fix now. Then you can keep going back to this list and work your way through the tips that resonate.

CHAPTER 6

Immediate Energy Boosts and Quick Fixes

I would like to help you find a structural solution for your lack of energy. But I also know we sometimes need quick fixes to tide us over and get us through the day. Here is a list of things you can use right away to boost your energy or support your state of mind.

For More Energy...

Diffuse lemon oil. Lemon is a powerful essential oil—great to boost your immune system and kill germs. So when my boyfriend had the flu, I diffused it in our bedroom during the day to expedite his recovery and to protect me. At night, I always turned on the diffuser before going to bed. I did the same that day, forgetting the apparatus contained lemon oil rather than my usual lavender blend. I didn't realize my mistake until we both lay awake for hours—tired but too energized to sleep. I've never forgotten the energy boost lemon oil gave us and have consciously used it ever since when needing extra energy.

Close your energetic circuit. For an immediate energy boost, place the top of your middle finger and the top of your ring finger against the tip of your thumb and do so with both hands. Make sure your fingers are touching but you do not need to exert pressure. This closes an energetic circuit in your body so the energy starts to recirculate. Sit like this for a few minutes. You may feel a tingling sensation, but even if you do not sense a difference it is still working. The first few times I did this exercise, it took several minutes for me to feel anything. You can continue talking to someone or watch TV, for example, while you do this.

Increase your oxygen. Yawning sends more oxygen to your brain and makes you more alert. You can also go for a walk and deeply inhale fresh air, or open a window to allow in more oxygen.

Call your energy back. See Chapter 12 for more information. Or go straight to the guided activation Call Your Energy Back on **www.radianttools.nl**.

For Better Focus and Concentration...

Diffuse lemon oil. Lemon is one of the most powerful essential oils when it comes to improving your concentration. Research in Japan showed that typists made up to 54% (!) fewer mistakes when lemon oil was diffused in the room. Lemon oil will help you clear your mind and focus. A few drops in a diffuser or clay stone on your desk will help you disperse this delicious fresh scent. Several Japanese companies are actively using the benefits of lemon oil and have built-in complete aromatherapy systems to improve productivity and accuracy of their personnel. I just put some lemon oil in my diffuser, and it immediately gave me a fresh and bright mood (while it also helped me write this text).

Ground yourself. Grounding will help you be fully present and more focused.

Diffuse rosemary oil. Rosemary has a stimulating effect on the central nervous system. It improves concentration and will help boost your energy. Rosemary will give you more physical and mental strength. Therefore, do not use this oil in the evening unless you plan on staying up all night. Rosemary enhances your alertness and will help you concentrate for longer stretches of time. Research where the subjects were exposed to three minutes of aromatherapy proved that rosemary improved and accelerated memory recall and ensured more alertness. Put a drop of this spicy and refreshing scent on a tissue or handkerchief so you always have some extra concentration at hand. Or to use the words of Shakespeare, "Here's rosemary, for remembrance…"

Diffuse peppermint oil. This refreshing essential oil helps clear your mind and enhances your concentration. Peppermint is also great when you are coming down with a cold or flu. It stimulates your immune system and helps expel mucous.

For Relaxation...

Use lavender oil. This is one of my favorite oils because it's so versatile. When you feel a headache coming on, massage one drop of lavender oil on each of your temples. This is calming and soothing, and helps alleviate your headache. For sleeping difficulties, diffuse lavender in the bedroom with an aroma diffuser or put a drop of lavender on a tissue next to your pillow or on your pillowcase. This will help you fall asleep and sleep through the night. You can also take a relaxing bath with lavender to usher in a good night's rest. Use no more than ten drops of lavender in a full bath for an adult. Always mix an essential oil with a neutral bath oil, shower gel, or other emulsifier, so the oil will not float on top of the water. You can also diffuse lavender oil in your study or living room to help you wind down and relax. What is unique about lavender oil (besides being one of the few safe oils to use undiluted on your skin) is that it is normalizing. This means when you are tired it will pick you up, when you are stressed it will calm you down. Like magic! I believe everyone should have a bottle of pure lavender oil in their home. I carry a bottle in my purse at all times. It helps with mosquito bites and even burns. When in doubt, use lavender essential oil. Just make sure it is pure lavendula angustifolia (without any other ingredients).

Ground yourself. Get back into your body and feel what it needs.

Do a relaxation meditation. This guided visualization helps you relax and release some of the tension you're holding in your body. The audio is available at **www.radianttools.nl**.

For Letting Go of Fear or Worry...

Shift your focus. When you are afraid or worried, it helps to shift your focus by consciously redirecting your attention to something else. Read a book, play your favorite music, dance, relax through using the power of your breath, call a friend. Basically anything else is better than wallowing in fear or worry.

Make a gratitude list. Write down five things you are grateful for and allow yourself to truly FEEL them. (See Chapter 24 for more tips on gratitude).

Smile! When you are worried or fearful it's important to step out of that cycle. Force yourself to smile. Pull the corners of your mouth up. Doing so releases happy hormones in your brain that will actually make you feel better. Your brain does not know you had nothing to smile about and believes you are genuinely happy and smiling. Before you know it you actually feel like you had a reason to smile! Even if it feels uncomfortable or awkward at first, stick with it, knowing you will feel happier shortly. Works like a charm.

Get a hug. If need be, give yourself a hug. Touch is so important. There is a reason we rub our knee after we've hurt it. Rubbing our skin releases hormones that make us feel better and lessens the pain. Family therapist Virginia Satir once said, "We need 4 hugs a day for survival. We need 8 hugs a day for maintenance. We need 12 hugs a day for growth." While that may sound like a lot of hugs, it shows why physical contact is crucial.

I recommend you do not use these shortcuts to patch the holes and not fix the underlying, true problem. I know life (and your body) will catch up with you if you do and you will regret not taking the foundational steps to shift to a state of true energy and balance. Having said that, please do use these practical tools to tide you over in your hour of need.

CHAPTER 7

Uplevel Your Self—Care

I truly believe this world would be a better place if we all knew how to take care of ourselves. We are often busy trying to fix others, but if we focused that energy and attention on ourselves—making sure we are healthy and sane and full of self-love— then there would be so much less to fix.

Many problems in the world stem from people who are unhappy or in pain, lashing out at the world and at other people in an attempt to feel better. A lot of problems arise from their crippled view of the world, of what it takes to give or feel love. Problems we would not have to fix if we focused more energy and attention on taking care of ourselves so we don't get derailed.

I'm not saying you can't reach out for support; in fact, you should—it's a sign of strength.

I'm not saying to be selfish and let other people rot in their misery.

I AM saying: learn to take good care of yourself, educate yourself about how to nourish your body, mind, and soul, how to engage in healthy relationships, and how to pursue a life that fulfills you and those around you.

If we all learn how to take care of ourselves first, we free up a lot of time and energy to do positive things rather than cleaning up other people's messes.

We can start living as examples of joyful, focused spirit. By tapping into our personal SWEET POWER™, we free up time and energy for growth, success, and love.

Life Is Meant to Be Enjoyed

I've had to work hard to get where I am. It took me countless years to learn to master my energy and handle my sensitivity.

I'll never forget the day I went to see a naturopath, after my "regular" doctors had been unable to figure out why I was so tired and exhausted for the past eight years.

When the naturopath's diagnosis only took thirty minutes, and his verdict was that I was surviving on willpower, which was damaging my organs, this was a giant wake-up call. That insight set me on a journey of discovering how to take better care of myself, how to set healthy boundaries, and how to actively manage my energy.

Because when you don't have the energy to enjoy life and do what you came here to do, then what's the point? I'm not here to work hard all day so I can go to bed early and do the same thing tomorrow. I want to be fully consciously present—not only be there in the flesh—so I can enjoy quality time with my friends and family, be happy and radiant.

I discovered that self-care is the key to everything and it saddens me that for so many people it is their last priority. This isn't wishful thinking or some "when I say it often enough it will happen" mantra.

Continue to monitor your energy level this week with the Energy Inventory Tool I gave you. Do this at least every morning and evening, but preferably during the rest of the day as well. This allows you to get a grip on, and feel for, your energy level and how it fluctuates throughout the day. It will give you an idea of what gives or costs you energy. Remember to ask yourself: am I grounded? Check in and if needed look at the checklist for signs and feel it in your body. If yes: ask yourself if you are FULLY grounded, to the max? Or can you take it a bit further?

Crucial Life Skill

I feel like self-care is getting a bad rap from being trivialized: *Feeling overwhelmed? Take a bath.*

By all means, do take a bath. Because it can be very relaxing, good quality time and exactly what you need to deal with the overwhelm in the short-term. But what I mean by self-care is learning how to inherently take care of yourself, because most of us have no clue. We are pushing buttons left, right and center in the hopes of hitting the right one. None of us have been taught or have taken the time to figure out what our body, mind, and soul actually *need* to be balanced. What helps us recharge and relax and stay sane? The only people who do know are the ones that were forced to learn because they were backed up against the wall by a burnout, accident, or intense life event. Like me.

I want you to know what to do *before* you get to that point. I want you to be able to steer clear from burnout before you have exhausted yourself, or before you have depleted your reserves and you feel the only way to survive is to quit your job or leave your partner because you barely have the bandwidth to think straight, let alone deal with another human being.

I've had clients come to me more than once, thinking they had to cut all ties with their spouse because this simply was not working for them. Then after they had taken all the steps they could to care for themselves so they were no longer drained, they realized there were a few changes to be made in the relationship, but that the changes were all doable. Often it's a matter of communicating one's needs. I've seen relationships flourish after clients learned how to give themselves what they needed in a balanced way. Giving yourself what you need does include asking for support—just to be clear.

I wish self-care was taught in school. I think it's a crucial life-skill along with many others, like learning how to grieve. That's what we need to know in order to have a happy, healthy, sane life. When I talk about self-care, I'm not speaking about frilly, optional, fluffy stuff. I'm talking about the foundation, knowing what you need in order to be balanced and fill up your tank with crucial information—so that you have the support to go places, to love your life, to fulfill your dreams, to support others, to connect, to be valuable, and to be able to contribute to the world.

True self-care is about knowing what you need to be balanced and how to recharge your body, mind, and soul. To recognize the need for time alone. To balance your life so you are not running on empty all the time.

Living a healthy life includes wholesome nutrition, plenty of physical exercise, and enough sleep. Though I am fully aware of the importance of regular exercise and the impact it can have on your energy level and well-being, I will not be covering that topic in this book since it is not my field of expertise. But I do hope you find a way to work out that fits your body and its needs and abilities.

> **TRUTH**: True self-care is the structural foundation on which you build your life.

It's more than a nice bath, candles, and turning in early for one night. True self-care is about healthy habits, underlying beliefs. and making yourself a priority rather than an afterthought.

That does not mean there will never be moments when you work through the evening because of a deadline or have to push through in some other way. Of course, life happens. But when you have a healthy foundation, those moments where you have to push through will not derail you as much. Because you now have both the tools and the bandwidth to be able to deal with that.

Self-Care Is Not Selfish

You know that airplane safety demonstration only a few people watch? When the flight attendant tells you to put on your own oxygen mask first, before assisting anyone else?

Well, that doesn't only apply to airplanes or emergency situations. In fact, I believe putting yourself first should be mandatory for the manual of life.

Because if you don't take care of yourself first, then how on earth will you have anything to give to others?

I know, I know.

You're doing your best to be a good parent, partner, friend, and colleague. How's that working out for you? You're running your own business or trying to keep all the balls in the air at work and at home. Because that's who you are.

You care, you want things to be done well—if not perfectly.

You have a full schedule and there simply isn't always time for what you want or need. You'll catch up with that on the weekend, or during that vacation—three months from now.

> **TRUTH**: We need at least one hour
> for ourselves Every Single Day.

One hour is the minimum allotted time humans need to be healthy and happy and sane. But most of us have trouble squeezing in thirty minutes of alone time.

It's something I struggled with for years. Because there's always more to do....

We have high standards for others, but even higher standards for ourselves.

We want to be productive with our time, have something to show for it. I know I feel good when I can rattle off a list of things I accomplished in a day.

What really matters is how that day felt. How *you* feel most of the time. Because that's what fuels you for the days to come.

About that hour of time for yourself? The trick is to do only things that bring you joy. No "useful" stuff is allowed during those sixty minutes. (Yes, more time is even better!)

This is your playtime. No working in the garden because you *almost* enjoy it. Walking the dog because it helps you get your 10,000 steps done doesn't count either. Nor does cooking, unless you take a class just for the fun of it.

Does that sound selfish? Or undoable?

It's all about knowing that when you *are* in a good place—when you have energy and enthusiasm because you took good care of yourself—you will be so much more fun to be around.

You will have the bandwidth to be flexible with your partner, your children, your colleagues. You will not get grumpy at the first sign of pushback. When you are relaxed you can see solutions more quickly; you are more productive and creative. See how that hour wins itself back?

Most of all, when you take care of yourself first, when you put on that oxygen mask way before there is ever an emergency landing, you will live in the flow. You will have a much happier, healthier life. Can you feel it?

Self-care is not selfish. It's smart! And it should be a priority rather than an afterthought.

Because you can't pour from an empty cup. If you're exhausted, you have nothing to give. You will be able to serve your family and clients better when you are in good shape—physically, mentally, and emotionally; when you have energy left over and can spend quality time or do something fun with friends and family.

Most sensitive people find it very difficult to do this. Because they are aware of everyone's needs, they tend to put other people first. You can't. Not if you want to stay healthy. As I said before, I believe the world would be in much better shape if everyone took care of themselves first. I'm not saying leave your children to themselves and let them figure everything out on their own. However, they do need to understand that you need time for yourself as well. It's a beautiful way to model that it is very healthy (and normal!) to take good care of yourself. They will see that it makes you happier, more energetic, and more fun to be around.

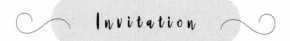

Invitation

Schedule at least thirty minutes (ideally one hour) of high-quality time for yourself today or tomorrow at the latest. Yes, I'm serious. If you can't find thirty minutes for yourself in these two days you honestly need to rethink your priorities. Rearrange your schedule if you need to, hire a babysitter, or ask someone to help if that's what it takes to give yourself that thirty-minute window.

I'm reminded of a private client who ran her own business. She reached out because she was exhausted and depleted. When I gave her this assignment, she genuinely struggled to find half an hour per day. Not just once but every day. It was a monumental task for her. But once we worked through the mindset shift that was required for her to start seeing possibilities and solutions rather than problems, she freed up so much time, energy, and joy.

CHAPTER 8

How to Handle Your Sensitivity

Up until my late twenties I did not see myself as a sensitive soul because I had unconsciously closed down part of my intuition, no doubt as protection to help me navigate life at the time. Plus, I did not know any better. This was who I was and I had no idea how things felt for other people.

I have cursed my sensitivity many times. It made me feel weak, vulnerable, and incompetent. Being highly sensitive meant I was unable to do things other people had no problem doing without getting exhausted. It meant I had to stay home because I was over-stimulated and needed some peace and quiet to make it through the rest of the day.

I remember one incident at a supermarket when I was young. We were on vacation in France, shopping for groceries, and I was pushing the shopping cart. After a few minutes my arms were in so much pain that I just couldn't push the cart anymore. I asked my younger brother to take over. He gave me one of those "here we go again" looks, making me feel like I was exaggerating things and being childish and lazy. I felt hurt and misunderstood. He thought

I was simply unwilling to push the cart. He thought I was making things up. After about half an hour the pain went away and I was able to use my arms normally, so I helped put the groceries in the back of the car. To my brother that was clear confirmation I had been pulling his leg and hiding out. I've had to hear this story over and over again. Every time I mentioned something wasn't feeling right or was difficult for me, he would holler, "Oh, here we go again, be careful or her arms will start hurting."

It made me feel alone. I felt like there was something fundamentally wrong with me. Many years later I finally understood what had happened. I must have picked up some energy from the person who had used the shopping cart before us. The effect on me was so immediate it had to have been from touching the cart. Perhaps they had a physical problem or maybe it was just their energy that felt so painful in my system. When it happened, I had no idea it was possible to pick up someone else's energy or emotion, and that you could feel actual physical pain from that experience.

For a long time I resented the way my brother had reacted. Until I realized that from his perspective it must have looked strange. It didn't fit anything he'd ever experienced. With hindsight I understood his response.

I've always known I was different than most people and to me it felt like a weakness, because it kept me from doing things. I stayed home the day after Christmas when everyone went on an epic hike in the Smoky Mountains. I knew I didn't have the energy to go—which is why I stayed home to read—but I didn't yet understand *why*. Which made it hard to explain, especially after seeing the pictures with ten-foot icicles and hearing countless times "You should've come, it was a once-in-a-lifetime opportunity!"

When I started to open up to my intuition I had no clue how to deal with my sensitivity. Nobody had taught me how to keep other people's emotions out of my system or how to know when my intuition was spot-on. Once I got a handle on my sensitivity, my energy increased and I felt so much better.

I learned to get a grip on my energy by grounding myself and then cleansing my energy field. I will show you how to do the latter in Chapter 12.

Managing Your Sensitivity

Being sensitive is great—it really is. It can be your superpower. But only if you know how to manage it. Otherwise it can drain you and make you feel like there's something wrong with you.

I know a lot of people are unaware of the impact being sensitive has on their lives. For me personally, it has been a struggle. At first I did not know my loss of energy was connected to being sensitive. I had to learn what to do differently to feel good about being sensitive, to have more energy, and not be overwhelmed.

> **TIP**: Avoid overstimulation

Since you are picking up pretty much everything that's going on around you, it's crucial to consciously build in time for yourself. Time to recharge and recoup from being overstimulated.

If you have not already scheduled time for yourself (remember the invitation from the previous chapter?) I recommend you do so right now. Pick up your calendar and plug it in. As a sensitive soul especially, you need one hour per day to yourself to stay sane and balanced.

Even if your day is swamped, I suggest you excuse yourself for a few minutes so you can take a breather. I guarantee you will feel a difference when you start to consciously carve out time for yourself.

Just to be clear—watching TV is not the best way to avoid stimulation. Read a book, take a walk or a bath, meditate, knit, paint—do whatever soothes you and makes you feel better. You will know which activities will help you recharge and which ones only drain you further. Using the Daily Energy Inventory will help clarify that more.

Don't worry if you did not get to your me-time on a certain day. Just try to schedule some time for yourself on the next day. It's important not to beat yourself up because chances are, you are being plenty hard on yourself already.

Embracing Your Sensitivity

Embracing your sensitivity is crucial. The challenge is that you often experience your sensitivity as something that's holding you back. It may feel like a burden, like it did for me. Even if you didn't know until recently that you were a sensitive soul, I would wager you have always known you were different and that might have bothered you.

> **TRUTH**: Your sensitivity is not a weakness or something you need to hide. You can stop feeling like there is something wrong with you.

I remember years ago at a training on Spiritual Psychology the host told me, "Iris, your sensitivity really is your strength."

I heard what he said and somewhere it resonated, but my mind was saying, "Excuse me? Do you have any idea how much trouble this has caused me? How weak it has made me feel? How can that possibly be a strength?" I could only see the limitations and what having no idea how to manage my sensitivity had cost me. I had no handle on it. My sensitivity was running me instead of the other way around.

Until I opened myself up to the idea that perhaps it *was* possible for my sensitivity to be my strength. That's when I began to discover how I could manage it. As soon as I started getting a grip on my sensitivity, I noticed the positives. Thanks to my extreme sensitivity I'm able to pick up on what is going on with other people's energy. It's what enables me to tap into intuitive insights, and bring through the healing energy someone needs.

I was finally able to sense what someone needed *without* being affected by it. I could provide clients with what they required without having to feel their pain and be burdened by their emotions. At long last I had turned my curse into a gift!

That's what I want for you, too. I want to help you see your sensitivity as a strength and a valuable tool that makes you unique and enables you to achieve remarkable results. This is what makes it possible for you to do what you came here to do. Even if you are not yet using it on a conscious level, it is what will give you a huge advantage and will make a big difference in your life. Even if it's "only" because it allows you to be more accurate and efficient in what you do, more intuitive and aligned.

Because sensitive souls are good at reading underlying dynamics in a team or organization, they are invaluable in teambuilding. Their ability to absorb more details often allows them to have a clear overview and to see connections. They might need a moment to process information, but when they speak up their input is usually spot-on. And in my experience sensitive souls are very creative—either with their hands or because they have a lot of (innovative) ideas.

It starts by allowing yourself to open up to the possibility that your sensitivity is something that could actually be positive. It doesn't matter if you have no idea what that may look like.

For me it's like a weird push-pull between "I guess everybody must be experiencing this," and "Why doesn't anyone else have this problem?"

For example, until the age of twenty-eight I thought everyone came home with an intense headache after shopping. On the other hand, most people did not appear to have a problem pushing shopping carts, or going to parties without getting exhausted.

This is my invitation to you: try to accept and embrace your sensitivity and start seeing it as your strength.

I believe there is a reason you are a sensitive soul, and it is not to punish or burden you. Your sensitivity enables you to do something you would not be able to do without it. You may or may not have discovered what that talent is, but it truly is vital.

I know this likely is a process that will take a while and I highly recommend you give yourself the gift of healing any scars your sensitivity might have given you. Simply knowing you are highly sensitive might have already solved a riddle and put you at ease. Speaking about it with friends and family may help, so they too can understand your needs and why you respond differently in certain situations.

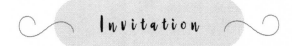

Invitation

Take a moment to think about what you are able to do thanks to your sensitivity. How are you serving your clients or supporting your colleagues and friends in a way that you would not be able to do without your sensitivity? How does being sensitive help you navigate situations because you "know" things or sense when someone is lying or uncomfortable? Write down anything and everything that comes to mind. Even if it does not yet make any sense. Just keep writing. Once you are done, I suggest you reread the list you made with an open mind and an open heart. Chances are there are some pieces in there you had not thought of before. Because it comes so naturally to you. You may not even be aware you are doing it.

If you are convinced you are not highly sensitive then I recommend you focus instead on other elements of yourself that you have difficulty embracing. What is a character trait, a habit, something that makes you uniquely you, that you have difficulty accepting? Can you look at that element through fresh eyes and see what might be its value? What did it bring you? What has it allowed you to do?

CHAPTER 9

Follow Your Joy

For years I tried to fit in and go with the masses. People told me to try harder or simply adapt. Even recently, someone very close to me said, "Yes, I know you are different, but you are the minority here so you can at least try to adapt to us."

What?! That's what I have done most of my life and that's what has made me miserable. Trying harder and pushing myself past healthy boundaries is NOT the solution for me! It isn't the solution for you, either.

What do they want me to say? "Yeah sure, let me just squash my feelings and needs. I'll be over in the corner feeling miserable. Don't bother on my behalf."

For me, it had gotten to the point where I was trying so hard to be someone I was not that my physical body could no longer keep up with me. I had to learn how to take care of myself both energetically and physically. And I learned it meant I had to do things differently than most people.

About 80% of the population is less sensitive, which means the way things are generally done—the way everyone is used to—is geared toward the majority. "The way everyone is used to" often does not fit me and probably does not work so well for you, either.

We just need other things than most people do to function well. More alone time, for example. When you plan your day and week, taking your sensitivity into account makes it much easier to avoid being drained from overstimulation. The Daily Energy Inventory will alert you to when you are doing too much and show you what a balanced day looks like.

Managing yourself, choosing who you are, what you want to be, and where you spend your time and energy has a lot to do with being true to yourself. To being authentic. To hold on to that authenticity despite what other people might think.

We often live our life backwards. We want to make a lot of money, so we can do more of the things we enjoy, and (we think) live happier lives. I believe we should start by doing more things we enjoy and less of what drains us or makes us unhappy. There is no need to wait until you have a certain amount of money to start working less and to be happier. You can be happier *now*!

Good self-care goes beyond rest and taking care of your physical, mental, and emotional well-being. I believe it should include looking after your own happiness. That is your responsibility. No one else's.

That means you need to get clear on what you need in order to thrive. Focusing on "not being drained" is not good enough. I want you to feel *amazing*. If you're doing soul-sucking work, if you're in a relationship that isn't working, it's your duty to change. Either focus on improving the relationship or move on. Same goes for your job. Life is too short to settle for anything less than what brings you joy. It might look like you don't have time to spare for fun. Joy might seem luxurious. But fun is a catalyst. What brings you joy is also your generator for more energy! And your happiness is definitely a prerequisite for becoming radiant.

> **TRUTH**: That which brings you the most
> joy is what will bring you the most!

One of my athlete clients has posted this coaching message on her mirror. As a result of keeping the pursuit of joy foremost in her mind, she shines.

I'm not saying you can't have bad days. But when you genuinely assess which actions and roles in your life are bringing you joy or draining you, you'll know in your heart whether the relationship, the job, the whatever, is no longer aligned for who you are and what you need.

Change is scary. People are creatures of habit. We often like a certain amount of predictability, some more than others. Change does not always come naturally. There is resistance because our mind wants things to be clear-cut and orderly. When we step out of our comfort zone, it will (by definition) feel uncomfortable! Do not let that hold you back.

It will cost you energy when you are not aligned in any part of your life. Staying in a situation where you are not aligned can be a conscious choice, or something that you have assessed as only temporary, but make sure you are aware of the misalignment, of how that impacts your energy level, and of how you feel.

Choosing Joy

The largest chunk of our time is spent on our job or business, whether it's a paid position, volunteer work, or caring for family. When something eats up a large part of your time and energy, you better enjoy the work you're doing. Seeing people wait until retirement to start enjoying life makes me so sad.

I was fortunate to grow up with a father who loved his marketing job. He worked long hours but was happy to do so. Even in retirement, he continues to offer his international marketing expertise through volunteering, assisting startups or businesses in need of support. For him it would be a punishment to not be allowed to do what he loves most. He watches more TED Talks than anyone I know and reads all the latest books on a variety of topics. That's his idea of fun.

His passion for marketing inspired me to follow in his footsteps. During school vacations, I sometimes accompanied him to work, which was especially fun when they were shooting a commercial. Seeing the variety of work included in the marketing department spoke to me. It felt like a place where I could use my creativity. After several years in my corporate marketing job, I felt a nudge to make a career change and I honored that suggestion, even though it was scary.

Making that change required me to release expectations (including my own). To let go of what I was *supposed* to be doing. To release myself from what was expected or logical, given my studies in Commercial Economics and my MBA. I had to give myself permission to pursue what brought me joy. You might also need a major change in your career focus or another key aspect of your life. But in order for you to be able to make that change, you need to get clear on what brings you joy in the first place.

I believe a lot of joy (and energy!) is to be found when you live your purpose. Ignoring or not recognizing your calling can be draining.

Discovering your purpose is a topic large enough to warrant its own book, but in order to get you pointed in the right direction, I ask you to become aware of what brings you joy and to follow that path. Trust where it leads you and even if it doesn't show you your purpose, at least you had a delightful time.

What makes you smile? Which activities light you up? What do you love doing most? Start jotting down a few answers that come to mind. Then look at how you can allocate more time to those activities. Perhaps you want to take a course to explore a certain skill, connect to like-minded people, or use more of your hours doing what makes you thrive—and shine.

Create a Healthy Morning Routine

Sometimes, finding authenticity and daily joy is in the little things. It took me some time to figure out the best morning routine for myself. I start with a large glass of warm water. I know this sounds dreadful to most people, but I assure you it's great. As I mentioned before, the body more easily processes liquids at body temperature. A morning glass of water replenishes fluids in the body lost through perspiration during the night and supports cleansing the kidneys.

As I'm waiting for the water to boil I ground myself, then cleanse and protect my energy (more on that later).

Then I drink a second glass of warm water with lemon and a teaspoon of honey (an Ayurvedic practice to clean the bowels). Afterwards I do my yoga, followed by either meditation or tuning-in. Sometimes journaling. One of my favorite parts is setting intentions for the day, followed by breakfast. As a rule, I don't see clients before 11:00 a.m.

When you're by yourself or with your significant other, it's relatively easy to gently commit to the morning routine that helps you become present and ready for a day in the flow. But on the days a cleaning lady came in, I noticed my morning activities took more effort. I felt odd sitting still and meditating on the couch while she was cleaning my office. I noticed my first instinct was to skip a morning. Until I caught myself: *It doesn't matter what she thinks, this is what I need.* She might find my routine strange, but that's no reason not to do it. I admit, the first time I meditated while someone else was present in the house did feel uncomfortable. I felt very visible. But I'm so glad I chose to be true to what I needed and not worry about what other people might think, because I know what a difference it makes in how that day feels.

Choosing to honor your own routine despite fears of what others may think might seem like a small thing, but self-commitment is where establishing your daily practice starts. It would have been easy to miss out on my meditation. I'm sure it would have sounded reasonable to anyone I told. But giving up my routine would have impacted the flow of my day. I would have sold myself short.

It's hard not to be bothered by what other people think. Self-consciousness impacts us much more than we want it to, and letting go of the fear of outside opinions is a process.

When you are feeling down or things are not going your way, staying true to yourself and your needs will be a bit harder. You have to be prepared for the difficult days. I find keeping in mind that some days will be challenging really helps. Gently remind yourself that finding joy and energy in your daily routine is a process, and sometimes it's harder to stay with it. And that's okay.

I invite you to embrace more of who you are so you can fully do what you came here to do in this lifetime, and to enjoy your life while you do that. It's not just about fulfilling a mission or making a living; I honestly believe life needs to be enjoyed. That joy will fuel you and make your life worth living.

Starting the day off on the right foot helps set the tone and energy for each day.

Invitation

What is your morning routine? Get clear on what works for you by trying a few things. For example, play with different workout routines. Do you like to go running, go to a gym, follow an online tai chi class, or walk the dog? Do you like peer support or prefer to be alone, focused on your own body? Explore forms of inner work like (guided) meditation, journaling, or breathing exercises. What helps you feel in tune and ready for the day? Find a breakfast that suits you and your body type by noticing how long your energy lasts after eating.

Establishing a healthy morning routine ensures you consciously start your day with a positive flow after some much-needed self-care.

Protecting your morning time might feel undoable, especially if you have children or a demanding job. Being my own boss helps me keep my routine. That doesn't mean you can't carve out fifteen minutes for yourself if you choose to. More often than not, your self-care depends on what you are allowing yourself, much more so than what is actually "possible." I've had to work through several mindset shifts, releasing limiting beliefs about what I thought I could do. About what it meant if I was not seeing clients until 11:00 a.m., for example. But I'm in better shape after I take the time for my morning routine and better able to support my clients as a result. In addition, I feel really good! It's win-win.

What can you do today or this week that's fun? That's just for enjoyment?

What I would like you to do this week is to take a look at the Daily Energy Inventory lists you made over the last few days or weeks. What stands out? Pick the five things that drain you the most and then decide which three you will stop doing or do less of. Or, if you really need to keep doing one, find a way to make that activity less draining. Then please share these three things you will stop or change with the people involved.

CHAPTER 10

Set Healthy Boundaries

At the start of this book I shared the story of my burnout. I was only twenty-four at the time. I realized I needed to change a lot of things about how I was living my life. It was not just about working fewer hours, but a complete overhaul of what I valued in life. My growth has been a process, but two things that have helped me immensely are setting healthy boundaries and learning to say "no."

One of the reasons why so many people have trouble setting boundaries is that you are trying to set an invisible line—imaginary to most people—and that makes it harder to know where the edge actually lies. For yourself and others. Things would be so much easier if you could touch the boundary and point at it when you are arguing with someone. *See? That's where my boundary lies. Now stop overstepping!*

Second, it's a line that marks your limit. Except your limit is not the same every day. The imagined line might stray depending on your energy level, your mood, your tolerance for that person or situation. When you are rested and in a good mood, your boundary (or limit) to loud music, for example, is much more lenient then when you are grumpy, have a headache, or are facing a deadline.

Plus, if *you* are not clear about your limit, then how can you expect anyone else to be?

I'm sure there are areas where you are crystal clear on what you do or do not want or accept. But I'm guessing when it comes to your energy and your time you may not be as strict or even clear on your needs. This is a great moment to start thinking about what it is you need, and your Daily Energy Inventory sheet will be helpful in pointing at a few things. I will help you identify some of your boundaries.

Clear signs you need to set solid boundaries:

* ✳ You find it difficult to say "no."
* ✳ You take care of everyone else before you start thinking of yourself.
* ✳ You feel guilty when you take care of yourself first.
* ✳ You accumulate weight as a form of protection.
* ✳ You experience a sudden loss in energy, making you want to take a nap.
* ✳ Sometimes, seemingly out of nowhere, it becomes very difficult to focus and concentrate.
* ✳ You experience mood swings or feel emotions that are not related to what you are doing.
* ✳ You feel miserable.
* ✳ You do not have quality time to yourself.

It's important to realize two people are needed to set and uphold a boundary. You need to set it. That also means you have to communicate your limit. You cannot blame someone for overstepping a boundary you have never clarified. Or be angry when someone crosses a line that in the past was never a problem.

You need practical as well as emotional and energetic boundaries in place in order to have a grip on managing your energy. The practical ones are usually the easiest to get clarity on.

At times you may even need to set a healthy boundary for yourself. Like deleting the phone number of that guy who broke your heart, no matter how much you wish he would come to his senses. Or resist buying that bag of chips, cookies, or whatever you know you should avoid eating. Not because of your weight, but because of your health. Because you know too much sugar gives you brain fog and you are working on a deadline. Like I am right now. I'm avoiding sugar more strictly to be sharper and more productive while I write this book. Too rigid? Perhaps. But I know I feel the difference, so it's worth the small price for me.

By the way, I'm thrilled about the ample options available when it comes to tasty cookies and the like without sugar or gluten. Way back when I had to go on a very strict diet to overcome my hypoglycemia, there was exactly one edible type of cookie that fit within the rules of no sugar, no white flour, no yeast. And don't make me talk about the bread. It had to be specially ordered and came in once a week. The bread cost a fortune and it was solid enough to break a window. I'm Dutch so I'm big on bread, and to have to eat that one type of bread for three solid years was worse than missing out on all the cookies, cake, and chocolate.

When you do not set healthy boundaries you take a risk:

* You will feel depleted and overwhelmed.
* You may be living someone else's emotions and feelings.
* There is no energy or time left for you (or for what is really important aside from you).
* You will have little energy left at the end of the day or week (making it harder to recharge your battery as you dip below the sacred 20%).
* You are cutting yourself short and sooner or later you will have to pay with your health or your happiness. Likely both.

Setting healthy boundaries means listening to what is true for you. It requires you to color outside the lines of what you are "supposed" to be doing; of the expectations you have come to believe are normal for others to impose upon you. Setting boundaries asks you to replace *should* with *want,* and to examine what you need to be happy, healthy, and thriving. What you need to feel love and to love yourself.

Give yourself permission to do what is right for you and make your own choices.

We do not set boundaries either because we have never paused long enough to figure out what we need, or we are afraid of what people will think. We want others to like us. I used to have very few boundaries in place, for both reasons. Once I became aware of what drained me, I had to set a lot of boundaries on what I did, with whom, and for how long. I decided to only see clients three days per week, deliberately freeing up time to create content and to continue educating myself. I stopped going to events solely because I was expected to make an appearance. And I ceased investing time in friendships that did not nourish me long-term. I no longer had a tolerance for chitchat, most of which at the time made me feel like the odd one out. I did it because the cost of *not* setting that boundary was greater than the risk of being perceived as strange or difficult. Only you can decide which is more important. Although I believe your well-being should always come first.

> **TRUTH**: You cannot hand out enough favors to make yourself feel worthy. Just like crossing your own boundaries to benefit others won't make you feel better about who you truly are.

Because feeling worthy comes from within. It's a belief; a knowing. Not something you acquire by action. There are not enough actions in the world to make you feel worthy. No matter how many times you say "yes" when you feel like saying "no."

Respect Your Own Boundaries

You can't expect someone to respect your boundaries if you don't respect them yourself. People will pick up on this without exception. If you are not firm about your boundaries, people will test you. Seriously. This pushback is valuable information. The resistance indicates that your new boundary is not yet firmly anchored (or clearly communicated). It's worth taking an honest look at why you are uncertain about establishing this line. Uncover what you are afraid of.

Remember to be kind and allow yourself space to adjust to the changes you are going through. It's okay if you don't get it right the first time.

When you communicate your boundaries to others it might help to explain why something is important to you or why you need that line in place. These can be boundaries with your clients: *you can reach me between 1:00 p.m. and 2:00 p.m.* Or with your spouse and children: *do not disturb me in my office or when I'm taking a bath.* Perhaps you are not seeing clients on Fridays or you avoid checking emails on your vacation. If so, make sure you truly do not look at your email.

Especially with loved ones, it pays to walk them through what setting this boundary will bring you, and what the benefits are for them. If you will be less grumpy and have more energy, they might have an extra incentive to stick to the new rules you are laying down.

Setting boundaries is a never-ending process. As you grow and change your boundaries will shift with you. Some might become stricter; others obsolete. The more you are in tune with your body, the sooner you will pick up on where you need to make adjustments.

The moment I started to set stronger boundaries and make firm decisions about what I was no longer going to be doing, people started to push back. Over time I learned this was a signal I hadn't been totally comfortable setting that boundary. I've set much harder boundaries later in life and no one ever commented on it because I stood fast in my conviction.

As I was learning to set boundaries, where I was normally always available to people—being the good girl—I remember one moment in particular. Someone, let's call her Sue, was hosting a party and I didn't want to go. I didn't really like Sue for several reasons, but mostly because she was draining to be around. And I hadn't yet figured out how to protect my energy from being sucked dry.

After declining the invitation, I got a phone call from someone else asking me if it was true I wasn't going. I confirmed. Then she started yelling at me. I had to hold the phone away from my ear because she screamed so loudly! I was making dinner and I thought, *What is happening?!* The things she said to me were atrocious. I was basically a terrible, selfish person who didn't care about anyone else.

Which is almost funny because caring too much is what had gotten me in trouble in the first place.

I'm proud I didn't cave. I didn't go to Sue's party, although I did feel a tad guilty, thanks to that "lovely" phone call.

So if you start to set (stronger) boundaries, do not be surprised when people don't immediately accept them. Stay true to yourself and what you need. Because you have nothing to give to anyone when your well is empty. Plus, it's no one else's business how you are spending your time and why.

A quick overview as a reminder:

1. Have boundaries in place.
2. Know what they are.
3. Respect them yourself.
4. Communicate them clearly and lovingly.

Do you have enough boundaries in place? Do you know exactly what they are? Are you clear on what you need and what does and does not work for you?

If so, are your boundaries where they need to be or can they be stricter? Do you need to communicate some lines more clearly?

Which new boundaries would serve and support you? In the coming days and weeks, allow yourself to gain clarity on new lines you might want to draw. Once you are clear, communicate them with the people who need to know.

The Art of Saying No

If you are a people pleaser, chances are you rarely say *no*. I honestly do not like the term "people pleaser" because it sounds so needy. But I can't deny that for a large part of my life, that is exactly what I was.

Wanting people to like you often indicates uncertainty and a lack of self-esteem. However, I think it is too easy to chalk it all up to that. Most people pleasers try to avoid conflict. They often care deeply for others and how they feel. And there is nothing wrong with that.

Except the part where you say *yes* because you want people to like you. That is not healthy or desirable. Very few people truly do not care what other people think of them, though some might act like they do.

The solution isn't to become indifferent. I believe it is about limiting the number of people whose opinion truly matters. In addition to this, you have to minimize the importance of what people think of you.

You can't lead your life worrying about whether people like you if you do not do this or will say that. Though in reality this is how most people pleasers operate. I'm not saying this to make you feel bad if you are prone to wanting to please other people, but to make you realize this is no way to live your life: letting others dictate what you can and cannot do. Unless you are a psychic and can read people's minds, you will not know for sure what they truly want, anyway. All you can do is guess and hope that whatever it is you have to offer is going to please them. I believe life is too short for that.

As I said, I have totally done that. I'm really good at sensing what other people need or want and I was used to giving it to them before they even asked. Very nice of me, right?

Except most people took it for granted. The thank-yous I was secretly hoping for—because that's the reward; to be seen and appreciated—rarely came.

I was so busy taking care of everyone else that I forgot to take care of myself. Not just with my burnout, but after that as well.

I already told you we need at least one hour per day for ourselves to stay happy and healthy and balanced. When you are always running around taking care of everyone else before you ever think of you, then you will never get to that hour.

In order to free up time, you have to start saying no to things you secretly do not want to do. To things that no longer feel aligned or to chores you never wanted to do in the first place.

You can say "No," with a smile on your face and love in your heart. When you do that, you can say pretty much anything to anyone.

Remember: you are not saying no to the person but to the question. A lot of people find it difficult to say no because they feel they are rejecting the person. When you say no, be really clear, both verbally and energetically, that your response is not against *them* but is just an answer to their request. They have the right to ask a question. You have the right to say, "No, thank you."

The problem with saying no is most receivers take it very personally. And it isn't. You setting healthy boundaries has nothing to do with how much you do or do not appreciate or like a person. Often the more emotionally mature and confident the other person is, the less chance there is of them taking your no personally.

When I started to tell family and friends I had discovered I was highly sensitive and very intuitive, I felt like I was coming out of the closet. I had always relied on my intellect; rarely had I consciously used my intuition, so it was a scary revelation. When I opened up to my intuitive abilities I became more sensitive as a result. Or, I should say, my sensitivity became more prominent once I was no longer squashing it. As a side effect, I was no longer able to be present in large groups without being wiped out. I was still figuring out how to set energetic boundaries. Some people thought I was being ridiculous, like the instance with Sue's party. Nonetheless, a handful were the best support I could have hoped for. My dear friend Elles is one of them. Her birthday was coming up. Picture forty people in a living room with little kids running around. A nightmare to the senses when you can't filter out all those impulses.

When I told her I couldn't make it to her birthday, she understood. I felt she truly meant it. She wasn't just being polite. We agreed to meet for tea the next day instead. We've been celebrating most of her birthdays, just the two of us, since. Elles was the first person who made me feel like it was perfectly fine to be myself.

Fair warning: when you are not used to saying no, you literally have to learn to say it. Which means you might be a little nervous to set that boundary. What often happens when you start saying no is that the first few times it comes out with a bit too much power. Like you have this hurdle to cross, so you gather a little extra speed to ensure you will be able to crest the hill. Then, once you do, you overshoot the mark and realize you did not need that much force.

That's okay. You're learning. You can apologize if needed and explain you're getting used to saying no. Often you have pent-up emotions and frustrations about all the times you said "Yes" when you meant "No" and that can add to the explosive nature of your first few nos. The more you do it, the more elegantly and subtly you will be able to communicate no.

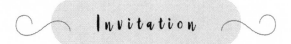

Invitation

Where can you start saying no? Think back to things you agreed to do that you regret. Now make a list of things you will start saying no to from now on.

Me-Time Is Sacred

The difficulty with me-time is that people often do not see it as occupied time. You have no appointment with anyone; you are not working or going anywhere. *Oh, you have time?* NO! It's interesting how some people believe they have a say in how you spend your own time.

An appointment with yourself is also an appointment; a very important one, I might add. This is something I learned thanks to a person who was very good at claiming my time. She seemed to have a sixth sense about knowing whether I had plans and if I didn't, she would ask me to do something or go somewhere. I would look at my calendar and see I had that time blocked off for myself. She would ask where I was going and with whom, was I working and on what? I was tempted to lie, and I admit at times I pretended I had to work when I knew I would be reading, because I realized she wouldn't take "No" for an answer if I had no good reason (in her opinion) to refuse. She excelled at making me feel guilty when I told her I would be taking me-time. So sometimes I pretended I needed to work because I had no energy left for a discussion on how I decided to use my spare time.

Just to be clear, she triggered something in me. She would not have been able to make me feel guilty if part of me didn't already feel guilty for saying no. For feeling like I was required to spend time with her or being selfish because I prioritized my self-care. In hindsight, it was a clear signal I hadn't yet fully integrated the knowing that my self-care was crucial and I would have nothing to give to others without it. Over time, I learned to say I wasn't available at a certain moment without explaining why (not just to her but in general). Because I don't need to clarify why I don't have time.

Creating me-time is one of the most difficult boundaries to set and protect. But it's definitely worth it because you'll get so much out of it! Expect a boost to your energy and productivity. You will get more done by taking some time off for yourself. I promise. There are times when things get so busy that before I know it old habits sneak up on me and I start working more without taking enough time to rejuvenate. And I pay for it by not being as focused and alert. Not so high in energy. Then I recognize that as a sign to shift back and take time off, even if it sounds counterintuitive to work less when you have so much to do.

Be Clear Where Your Responsibility Begins and Ends

The advantage of being a sensitive soul is your ability to pick up on things other people might not notice. This also has its downside. Being able to feel what someone else might need does not mean you are the one who needs to provide it or solve the problem. The fact you are able to pick up on something does not make it your responsibility.

To get clarity on whether or not this is something you want to take on, ask yourself:

1. Is this my responsibility?
2. Does it have to be done now?
3. Am I the one who needs to do it, or can I delegate or outsource it?

Try to answer these questions honestly. That may be difficult at first because you are so used to solving everything for everyone. Chances are you have already taken action before you thought of answering these three questions. And that's okay. As with all these topics, this is a learning process. If you did dive in head first you can still ask yourself these questions afterwards, so you can learn from it moving forward.

If you do answer yes to all three questions, I recommend finding a way to make the thing you now have to do less draining or more pleasant.

In my previous home I had quite a few hedges in the garden and they grew like crazy. They had to be trimmed three or four times per year, which was unusually often. I don't like trimming borders. Or, I should say, I don't like cleaning up after because all the bending and standing gives me head rushes which makes me exhausted. At one point, I realized that even though it was my responsibility to ensure the boxwoods were in shape (I didn't want it to grow into a wilderness), I could hire a gardener. And it felt great.

Another thing to keep in mind when it comes to responsibility is whether you are actually doing this person a favor by helping them. You might be surprised that there are many instances where the answer will be no. It's noble you want to assist, but there are two things to keep in mind:

Do you want to help because you like to feel needed?

In truth, a lot of people do. No need to beat yourself up if this is the case. You're gathering valuable information and it's important to be aware of how actions are related to your self-esteem. This ties to an underlying belief that being needed makes you a better or a more valuable person. The truth is, your self-worth does not depend on that. Even though it may feel like it does. This is one of the things I support people with in my individual programs.

Am I serving this person by fixing this or that for him/her?

Are you doing them a favor or is it better if they figure this out on their own? Take a moment to sense that. Your intuition will probably tell you the answer if you let it. Sometimes people need to hit that brick wall. I know that it's devastating to watch, but there are times when we only prolong the inevitable if we keep fixing things for the ones we love. Be honest about whether it serves them better if they have to do this on their own. That doesn't mean you can't provide assistance or support, but they must do the lion's share. Make sense?

When my boss was transferred, a lot of her work ended up on my plate. I saw it as my responsibility to do it all, because it "had to" be done. In my eyes, doing less than a perfect job was not an option. Neither was saying "No." In hindsight, I should have sounded the alarm bell much sooner. I thought I was being a good employee by sticking it out, but I did both myself and the company a disservice by running myself ragged.

Stepping Out of Your Comfort Zone

As you are going through these exercises, you are stepping out of your comfort zone and embracing change. When you step out of your comfort zone it is uncomfortable by definition. Do not worry if you feel some (inner) resistance to making some of these changes. See it as a sign that you are stepping into uncharted territory. The unease is a way for your body to let you know you are venturing into the unknown. Your mind wants to keep you safe, hence the penchant for familiar things. I find it helpful to thank my unrest. *Thank you for letting me know, but I choose to do this.*

Whether something is a seemingly small step or whether it feels like a huge leap does not really matter. What is relevant is you decided to move forward and did not want to stay where you were. Because change can only happen *outside* your comfort zone.

By picking up this book you have shifted what you are willing to settle for. These practical steps allow you to move closer to who you really are and to learn to feel good about that. This stirs up things that may feel scary. You have embarked on a powerful journey and I hope you will remember change usually does not happen overnight. More often than not it's a process. I keep saying that. With good reason. I often have to remind clients they are making great progress even though not everything is the way they want it to be. If it were an easy shift, you would have made it ages ago.

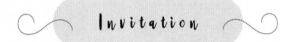

Invitation

Where are you taking on too much responsibility, or for whom? Keep this question in mind in the coming week. You might get clear on a few things you can stop doing or start doing differently. Or realize where it might not be in your (and their) highest good for you to do something.

CHAPTER 11

Surviving the Holidays

Halfway through Christmas dinner, I had developed an intense stomach pain. I had to push back with one hand against my abdomen while leaning with the other on the table, bent forward to somehow stay seated.

This wasn't new in itself. Most dinners ended up like this, for me.

Even though I enjoyed the company, I knew most likely I would end up feeling miserable. I simply assumed it was the food. Though I'm not a big eater, I might have eaten more than usual. Or perhaps it was the difference in cuisine....

It never occurred to me that the problem wasn't the food, but the energy and the emotions of the people around me. Or more precisely: I was unaware of how much those impacted me.

Since I'm super sensitive, I suck up other people's emotions like a sponge. I siphon their sadness, frustration, or stress, and everyone around me will feel fine. Much better, most likely. While I, on the other hand, will feel drained.

Sound familiar?

I've suffered through many dinners feeling exhausted—needing most of the next day to recharge and recoup. It wasn't until I learned how to take control of my energy and take care of myself that I was able to truly enjoy Christmas dinners or to be in large groups without being miserable.

I'm so glad those days are behind me, but I still remember how overwhelming it was. If you have ever felt miserable being in a large group of people—no matter how much you love them—that might be due to your sensitivity, as well. There is nothing wrong with you. You just have not yet learned how to take care of yourself, a skill I frankly believe should be taught in school.

I know the holidays can be exhausting. Not only because we usually put a lot of pressure on ourselves to get things done as perfectly as possible, but also because it often means spending large chunks of time with a lot of people. Whether or not you love them to pieces, it can still be draining.

Here are my best tips to help you get through the holidays (or any large gathering) with a lot more energy than usual. If you apply these three tips, I guarantee you will feel much better and will have more energy.

Survival Tip 1:
Schedule Time for Yourself

Especially when you are not used to being surrounded by people all day, this is a crucial tip. Even if you think it will not be much busier than on most days, I recommend you try this. It is so easy to get overstimulated by everything that is going on. Especially if you are a sensitive soul, this is crucial.

During the day, make sure you have some time to yourself. Whether it is sitting on the porch for a breath of fresh air, taking a short walk around the block, or hiding yourself in the attic to read a book or do a mini-meditation. As long as you choose to do something you enjoy.

If someone insists on joining you on your walk, perhaps suggest you walk in silence. Having some time to yourself is crucial. Your system needs to catch up from the constant overload of impressions so you can regroup and be ready for the remainder of the day.

I believe a lack of time on your own is one of the main reasons big holiday arguments and irritations occur. If you are overstimulated, there is no breathing room and it is so much easier to "snap" when Aunt Lynne annoys you or when another family member oversteps an invisible boundary.

Survival Tip 2:
Immediate Energy Boost to Keep You Going

You may reach a point where you notice your energy level starts to drop. Whether that is due to the amount of people surrounding you, the constant chattering, the temperature in the room, or the fact that it's getting late at night does not really matter.

This tip works anytime, anywhere. You can even do it while talking to your favorite aunt. I already mentioned it in the quick fixes section but I will happily remind you here.

∽ EXERCISE ∾

Place the top of your middle finger and the top of your ring finger against the tip of your thumb and do so with both hands. Make sure your fingers are touching but you do not need to exert pressure. This closes an energetic circuit in your body so the energy starts to recirculate. Sit like this for a few minutes. You may feel a tingling sensation, but even if you do not feel anything it is still working.

Survival Tip 3:
Guided Visualization to Release the
Day and Other People's Emotions

During the day it can be easy to gather emotions and energy from the people around you. Especially when you care for people and when they share things that might be emotional, it is easy to "pick up" some of their energy and unconsciously carry that with you. Even when you are not aware of it, it can still weigh you down.

You know the feeling when you get into a room and you sense people just had an argument? That's what happens in the energy and most of us carry some of that with us. Those energies stick to us like glue. This exercise will help you release the emotions and energies (good or bad) you picked up during the day. Because these are not your emotions and, therefore, they do not belong in your system. Chances are you will feel much lighter after this exercise, sensing a weight has been lifted from your shoulders. You will feel a difference in your energy level, too.

Listen to the Energy Cleansing Waterfall audio at **www. radianttools.nl**. This is a great way to end your day and "wash" everything away, so it is easier to go to sleep. Of course, you can do it during the day too.

Keep these tips in mind for the coming holidays or any large get-together so you can enjoy being present while taking good care of yourself.

CHAPTER 12

Supporting Your Energetic Body

Taking care of your energetic body, your aura, is just as important as taking care of your physical, emotional, and mental well-being.

For years, I was unaware of this. I barely knew I *had* an energetic body. It was not something anyone I knew spoke about. Once I learned more about being a sensitive soul, I understood why large groups of people often drained me. Or why I sensed other people's emotions.

There are four basic principles to be aware of:

1. Cleanse your energy.
2. Protect your energy.
3. Call your energy back.
4. Stop giving your energy away.

When you consistently apply the techniques explained below, you will free up a lot of energy and stop wasting it.

Cleanse Your Energy

We all pick up energies and emotions from other people. Sensitive souls more so than others. Because we can sense a misbalance in someone we often automatically start to correct that unbalance. Sadly, that generally means we take that negative energy from someone else and put it in our own backpack. Where we forget about it until it starts to bother us.

Have you ever heard people say they feel better when you are around? This is why. You help them unload negative emotions and energies. No wonder they felt lighter and happier when you paid them a visit.

When you siphon some of their emotions or energies it doesn't mean you take away all of it. Usually you take the edge off—which will help them feel better, but adds unneeded burden to your own stack. If you didn't have room for someone else's stuff to begin with, you might both end up feeling drained—because the amount you (unwittingly) took from them doesn't do enough to alleviate their overburden.

In principle, there is nothing wrong with helping someone re-find balance. As long as you remember to not take that energy on for yourself!

You can also take on energy from places. Especially if people just had an argument or if something bad or sad happened in a certain location. You might pick up on it by sensing something is off.

Since most sensitive souls unconsciously walk around like an energetic vacuum cleaner, it's essential to cleanse your energy field daily. There are several ways to clean your energy.

When you take a shower, you can imagine the water sweeping away all negative energies. Picture it going down the drain, the water taking with it anything that is not yours.

Even more powerful is the guided visualization Energy Cleansing Waterfall I mentioned in the previous chapter. You can find it at **www.radianttools.nl**. With this audio, all you have to do is sit back and listen while I steer you through this exercise.

Protect Your Energy

You have to stop taking on other people's emotions and energies. At one of my workshops a girl said, "When I get back from a party, I just need to cry first." For her, that's simply how it was. Crying was her way of releasing the emotions she had picked up at the event.

Often when people get exhausted from being in groups, like I was, they believe this is the price they have to pay. I want you to know there are things you can do about this. I'm not saying you can go to a party every night and not get tired, but you can go and manage your energy and sensitivity and the level to which you pick up things.

It's important to learn to distinguish between what is yours (emotions, energy) and what is someone else's. When you pick up on other people's emotions you might feel sad or angry for no apparent reason (other than that you encountered a sad or angry person and took on their stuff).

Draw the Energetic Curtain

Sometimes you can sit next to people that have yucky energy. I know you're not supposed to say that but some people can really zap your energy. That can be due to all kinds of reasons, and most of them don't do it on purpose.

⌒ EXERCISE ⌒

An easy way to keep other people's stuff out of your system is to draw an energetic curtain between you and the person you are sitting or standing next to. Imagine closing a curtain between you, and that curtain magically keeps their energies on their side and your energy on yours. This is one of the first things I do on an airplane or in a meeting.

This exercise works like a charm. Set the intention that this energetic curtain keeps your energy clean. There's no need for you to walk around with a lot of emotions and (negative) energies that are not even yours to begin with.

Often people think protecting their energy means putting up a brick wall between themselves and others. Some people do that when it comes to emotional things. They create a wall around their heart. Others do it for everything or anyone who gets too close, and that's why some people are hesitant to open up their heart.

However, an open heart does not equal an open energy field. Your aura is yours and yours alone. It's great to connect to others but there's no need to give them free rein in your energy field. Just like you would not give everyone the key to your home, either. Except with your energy, it's less tangible and less conscious.

Call Your Energy Back

This is especially vital for control freaks and perfectionists. Because there is something important you need to know about energy and how we operate. When we want to control something, we leave a little bit of our energy behind.

Often when we're feeling dispersed or scattered it's because we are. We have literally dispersed ourselves—left so much of our energy behind here and there—that we are not operating to our full extent or with our full power.

When you are feeling tired or exhausted, your first course of action should be to call your energy back. Assuming you are already grounded and have cleansed your energy.

Get your energy back from all the places you have left some behind in an attempt to soothe your mind—thinking it is in control.

By (unconsciously) attempting to control a certain outcome, you have used some of your life-force energy to try and influence the situation. That means this energy cannot be used for what it is intended. Your life force needs to be called back to your physical form so it can sustain what it is meant to sustain. Namely, you.

How do you do that? I've got you covered.

I have created an energetic activation to help you call back your energy and have more energy instantly! You can listen to Call Your Energy Back here: **www.radianttools.nl**.

Stop Giving Your Energy Away

Some people unconsciously give their energy away to others. Without knowing, they act like an energetic gas station. Though that is very kind, it's not a healthy habit. Your energy is meant for you alone. It's time to become fully aware of what you do with your energy. The Daily Energy Inventory can help you with that. If your energy goes down after meeting people—even when you had a good time—you might be handing out energy like free candy.

Being around people will always cost sensitive souls energy because you have to process all the extra stimuli. But if you are flat-out drained then you either need to limit your time in groups until you get a handle on your energy or stop giving it away. Or both.

You might notice your energy goes down more after seeing certain people. Unless they are going through a big life event (which is a normal reason for being lower in energy), these people might be the energy suckers. They excel at knowing where they can stock up on energy. Rather than organically increasing their own energy, they use you as an energetic gas station. More often than not they are not consciously aware of what they are doing, but that does not make their habit any less annoying.

Get clear on which people drain your energy. Maybe you noticed some on your Daily Energy Inventory sheet or you can just name a few. Then set boundaries. Perhaps limit the amount of time you spend with them, take extra energetic precautions, closely monitor your energy level and when it gets too low, get out of there or take a break.

I truly hope you will apply these simple but powerful tips. They have made a huge difference for me and I feel so much better when I consciously use them.

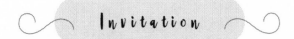

Invitation

Play with all the tools mentioned above. I recommend cleansing your energy at least twice a day, every day, after you have grounded yourself. This ensures you start your day and your night free from the drain of other people's emotions and energies. Then follow with protecting your energy field every morning and every evening. Use the other practices as needed.

CHAPTER 13

Make a Structural Shift

True self-care is a structural shift. It's making the decision that nothing is more important than YOU, and knowing you will not have anything to give to others when you are exhausted and overburdened. The next step is taking an honest look at your life and realizing where you can make changes.

You do not solve anything by going to bed early one time when you are drained. Making a structural shift is about fundamentally doing things differently; making conscious choices, setting new priorities—and knowing why that is important. Proper self-care is a systemic transformation of a new balance over the days and weeks. For some of you, it may be a complete overhaul of your habits and beliefs.

Keep an eye on the end goal: being happy and healthy and full of energy so you have time and drive left for the things that matter most to you, so you can become radiant and love your life. Allow yourself to take small steps. You don't need to change everything at once.

When I only had my Flowerdoctor website with the line of essential oil essences I had created, I checked my email every single day. I read my email on weekends, Christmas, New Year's Day, and on vacation. Because I was afraid of missing an order or disappointing a customer. I did that for two and a half years—over 900 days!

Until I booked a trip to Tuscany for a week with my family. Something made me decide I was going to do things differently this vacation. Tuscany is one of my favorite places in the world. The surroundings soothe me and it works wonders for my energy. Not to mention the cute historic towns and divine Italian food. At the time I didn't yet have an assistant, so the only solution was to turn on my out-of-office notifications to inform customers about the delay in response and delivery.

The first day I felt bad, like I was cheating or cutting class. Until I made the conscious decision to prioritize my health and well-being. To trust that whoever emailed me that week would understand, and if they didn't, a new customer would come in their stead.

I didn't look at my email once; I never even felt the desire to after I made that choice. I can barely begin to tell you what that week off did for my body, my mind, my sanity. I felt my body relax in places I hadn't realized I was holding tension. I felt freer, calmer, clearer. I had forgotten what that felt like. To not have to do something every day; to not be responsible or busy all the time. To rest my mind. That's when I vowed, "Never Again." When I'm on vacation I don't read email as a rule. I hired an assistant my clients can contact for emergencies. I know I can't do this intense work without taking extremely good care of myself. Hence I do. Not just for my clients, but for me and my family.

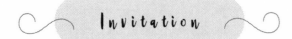

Invitation

Do you read mail on vacation? On your next vacation try to turn your email off. Perhaps delete it from your phone so you can't be tempted to take a peek.

Focus on You

What if today you focused on yourself first and foremost? On what YOU need. On what will help YOU shine and feel better. That's where it all starts.

Most people think taking care of themselves is optional. That it's for when you have time left over, not when you are pressured or burdened by your to-do list.

It's the other way around. The ONLY WAY to succeed in a healthy, wholehearted way is to start every day by taking inventory:

How do I feel?

How much energy do I have?

What will help me be more focused, grounded, connected?

If you take the time for that you will fly through the rest of your day because you will be in the flow. You might even have time to spare, time you would never have if you started with your to-do list and only used any "leftover" time to take care of yourself.

As I said, self-care is not selfish. It's smart!

Get other people on board with your self-care. Talk to your partner, family, and friends. They might be thrilled you brought it up. Explain which changes you want to make and why. They may need to learn how to take better care of themselves as much as you do. Help them understand why it is important for your health and sanity, and how they will benefit as well.

Ask them to respect the time you carve out for yourself, even if they do not fully understand it. Who knows? They might get inspired to try a few things for themselves. If your family and friends think you're going overboard with your self-care you might have to show them how exhausted you are. Or how much you yearn to do a few things for yourself. Usually our loved ones have no idea how much we struggle because we have never told them. And if after all that they still do not understand, ask them to support you with this simply because it's important to you.

A lot of the time we do not ask for what is really important. Setting healthy boundaries and taking good care of yourself does not only mean knowing what works for you, but applying it—and making sure you have the time and space to do that. Which might involve asking for help. Your future self will thank you for it!

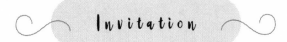

Invitation

Schedule a conversation with your loved ones about your self-care and the changes you intend to make. Remember to explain why it's important to you (and how it may also benefit them). Ask for their support as you embrace a new way of taking care of yourself.

The Inner Creates the Outer

The majority of results stem from our energy, not our actions. I believe the 80-20% rule applies here as well. I know that's not how most of us behave, nor is it what we've been taught. Instead, we spend the majority of our time taking frantic action to try to influence the remaining 20%. We like taking action after action, checking things off our to-do list. Doing so makes us feel like we are accomplishing things. It's the way we grew up, how we're educated, and how our society operates. You get rewarded for taking action, not for doing inner work or setting intentions. Focusing on your energy works; it truly does.

> **TRUTH**: Once you shift your energy, *everything* changes.

You need to remember you're a human BEing. Not a human DOing. And shift your attention accordingly.

Your focus first and foremost needs to be on your inner state of being and how you reflect that back into the world. Everything you send out will be returned to you tenfold. Scrutinize your thoughts and your way of being in the world.

Be ruthless when it comes to being aligned.

If the inner creates the outer, if 80% of our results stem from BEing rather than DOing, then what could possibly be more important than being in touch with yourself, your heart, your desires, your soul?

Rather than running around being frantic and busy, shift your focus to your inner well-being and get in sync with the flow.

Because when you feel aligned with who you are and what you need, you will not waste time. When you are in tune with your body, you effortlessly make the best decisions and you know what will support you and what will drain you. When you create from the heart you automatically do what is in your highest good—and that of those around you.

Now, how do you make that shift from 80% DOing to BEing 80% of the time?

It's a process, and do not let anyone tell you otherwise. There is no quick-fix magic button.

I know we all want things to change in an instant, but even when they do it's an accumulation of everything you've done up until then. You have merely reached the tipping point and that's when the change becomes visible.

The first step is becoming aware that your inner actions create outer results. Then shift your behavior to include more time for inner work. Managing your energy pays off—big time.

It took me a while to change my morning routine to include my daily yoga and energy work, which meant I would only start seeing clients at 11:00 a.m. At first it felt lazy, like I took the morning off.

Then I realized it made a huge difference in how I feel, in how present and alert I am. Doing my inner work in the morning increases my creativity and productivity.

The key is working smarter—not harder—using the principles you know yield results. Everything is energy so let the energy work *for* you so you can create from flow instead of a standstill. As I mentioned before, when you are in the flow actions and ideas fall into place and there's a perfect timing and synchronicity to everything that happens in your life

It's called inner WORK. Not inner play. Although we treat it like a luxury or something we do once we have time—after taking care of everything that is really important (or so we think).

My suggestion is to fit your inner work in first, so you know you'll get it done. You'll know you have created the space and the time to not only take care of yourself, but those around you, by making sure you are centered and focused, your energy is clear, and your emotions are gathered. By reminding yourself your energy is what has the biggest impact on any outcome—not your actions.

I know I am calmer, sharper, and more in the flow when I have done my inner work. When for whatever reason I do not get to managing my energy and state of being in the morning (because stuff happens), I can feel the difference and I am less productive.

If inner work is (or seems) impossible to fit into your mornings, then try to squeeze it in around lunch or mid-afternoon. Just make sure you fit it in somewhere, because shifting your energy will make a difference—I can guarantee you that.

If you leave your inner work 'til the end of the day, chances are you will be too tired and just want go to bed. Deciding to leave it until tomorrow when, for sure, you will do it then (or so you tell yourself).

Invitation

Do you want to make this your best year yet? Then incorporate some form of inner work into your daily routine so you can start your day from flow, making sure your energy reflects what you want to create and attract.

Use Your Time wisely

Deep inside sometimes you can feel a knowing, a hint of something your mind can't comprehend but that you know nonetheless. This is what I would call eternal wisdom or universal wisdom. A soul-connection to something that transcends time and space.

"There are more things in heaven and earth, Horatio,
* than are dreamt of in your philosophy."*
—*Hamlet*, William Shakespeare

This connection to universal wisdom has existed through all times. Except now the Internet makes news so accessible that it's easy to get bombarded and overwhelmed. When painful and sad things happen on such a grand scale and we learn news from other countries in just a matter of minutes—it's harder to maintain that connection.

We now have to deal with not only so much more information, but so much more misery as well. We take this in not only through words, but often accompanied by (intense) images on the news. I stopped watching the news long ago. Hearing about it is often bad enough; I don't need the visuals to imprint it even further. The same may go for you. What do you spend your time and energy on and how much of that is truly positive and uplifting? What helps you (re)connect to yourself and others, and what fosters a disconnect?

Nowadays, it's both so much harder and so much easier to be balanced. Harder because the increasing turmoil on the planet can take you off course, and the Internet is full of sad stories. Easier because you have unlimited access to self-help tools and uplifting inspiration.

The question is: what do you do with your time and how do you use your energy?

When you come home after work, how do you choose to spend the time you have? Do you pick nourishing activities that feed your body, mind, and soul? Or do you deplete yourself further by what you watch or read or do? Or feel you *should* do?

This is your choice and you are the only one who can answer this question honestly. In my experience, most of us could make wiser choices than we currently are. Most of us have much to gain from choosing with our heart and with love for ourselves. To listen to that universal wisdom or inner nudge. To commit to fewer obligations and more long-term investments in our health and well-being. It does not always show in the short-term but in the long-term we pay for depleting ourselves, and for disconnecting from our inner wisdom, ourselves and each other.

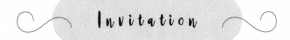

Invitation

Time is our most limited resource. This is your chance to choose wisely and take a moment to pause and ask yourself, *What do I need? What does my body need?*

I recommend you listen to the answer and take it seriously. Chances are you can already name a few things you know are not in your highest good. Take at least one action that supports the insights you just received. What will you change in your schedule or behavior that reflects a smarter, more aligned choice?

CHAPTER 14

The Labyrinth of Limiting Beliefs

You might not realize the deeper self-care needed in addition to getting a facial, taking supplements, or working out. These things are important maintenance and help you feel good about yourself. They are usually easier to schedule, partly because they are more widely accepted. People will not question your need for a haircut or dental visit. They might push back on seemingly less crucial forms of self-care—the ones that are less tangible but no less important. It's the change in your energy level that matters.

I don't believe your lack of self-care is because you are not aware of its importance or because you have never considered it or perhaps even tried it. I think there is an underlying reason why you are not putting your self-care knowledge into action. Sure, part of that might be lack of clarity on how much you actually need it or how to put certain things into practice. However, underneath that is a deeper layer. There is a fear or a belief that is stopping you from taking good care of yourself. And it's time we take a look at that.

It's interesting that something so seemingly logical as taking care of ourselves often takes a backseat. Self-care is one of the areas that triggers a lot. It's right up there with self-love and money. When it comes to putting ourselves first, a lot of underlying patterns emerge.

Patterns, (unconscious) beliefs, and behaviors are shaped by our past. They are formed by the unwritten rules of the families we grew up in, our society, our country, our friends, and our experiences. Some patterns are obvious, but the most important ones are sneakily riding in the back of our mind. Steering our actions and behavior, limiting what we think is possible or allowed.

There are so many "shoulds," especially for women, that it pays to take a hard look at your (unconscious) beliefs and the habits you are dutifully carrying around and acting upon.

I invite you to read through the following list and mark the statements you recognize. Please note, I said "recognize." That does not mean you agree with the statement, simply that you see yourself doing or thinking this from time to time.

* I'll finish this first and then I'll take a break.
* Am I worthy (enough)?
* Isn't that selfish?
* What would so-and-so think?
* I don't have time for that.
* I'll relax on the weekend or when I'm on vacation.
* Well, no one else is doing it.
* I don't need a break, I'm fine.
* Who am I to do/think/say that?

These are the more common beliefs and behaviors which cost you energy and hold you back. Almost always these beliefs are based on a fear of what might happen when you act a certain way.

My fingers are itching to dive in deeply and help you unravel each of these statements. But I promised this would be a book about energy management. (Plus my editor might kill me if I make this the size of a phone book!) When you recognize one or more of these limiting beliefs and behaviors, I recommend you start working on them. Releasing and shifting these beliefs is not something you get done in an afternoon and you will probably need support from a coach or mentor. The process is going to be a journey, but I promise you it will be worth it.

Having said that, there is one behavior I will unravel a bit further because it has played a huge role for me and it took me forever to uncover.

Toning Yourself Down

Those sneaky, less-visible beliefs often have to do with toning ourselves down. This is a belief I know intimately and have exercised for a very long time.

Because when you do not take super good care of yourself, you will be less productive, creative, and effective. As a result you will be less present, less grounded, and YOU WILL SHINE LESS!

Not giving yourself what you need to flourish is a great way to tone yourself down. Subconsciously, you are afraid of what will happen. Your mind is sublime at coming up with seemingly reasonable excuses why this is an exception or why you are doing something "only this once." In fact, the mind is so brilliant it can be hard to catch yourself in the act of undermining your health and well-being.

Does that sound familiar?

Take a moment and tune into your body—just sit and breathe—and ask yourself, *Could it be possible that not being super fit or full of energy is an unconscious way to hold myself back?*

Notice what happens in your body. Does it feel expansive or do you contract? Do you feel cringy or relaxed?

Do not judge yourself. We are simply gathering information. Allow yourself to be curious about the answer. I know it was true for me.

Contraction, cringing, or nervousness shows you are limiting the flow, which means you are indeed holding yourself back. When you connect to this question and you feel completely relaxed and at ease, you are probably not toning yourself down. Or at least not through a lack of self-care.

There are many possible reasons why you would want to tone yourself down:

* ✳ You are afraid of failure (and if you have not given it your all—because you did not have the energy to go full-out—then it is not as bad if you fail).
* ✳ You do not want to outshine anyone (most likely a sibling, parent, or caretaker).
* ✳ You are afraid to become visible.
* ✳ You prefer to stay small and safely in your comfort zone.
* ✳ You think you are not ready to step up.

Do any of these resonate? If so, you're not alone. I've had to face some hard truths about what I've done to sabotage myself at times. And I've seen it with a lot of my clients.

When it's hard to take good care of yourself, these fears might be at play. The good news is you're now aware and can start the work to shift and release these fears.

Here are my three best tips to deal with fear:

1. **Expect it.** Know that fear is a part of life. Feeling fear is often a sign that you are stepping out of your comfort zone and your ego mind is trying to get you back to familiar (thus "safe") territory. If you are prepared for fear, you can start to see it as a sign of change. Every time you do something new, whether it's in your personal or professional life, you can expect fear to rear its ugly head. Don't worry, it's supposed to.

2. **Accept it.** Try to embrace fear as a signal of new things coming your way. Your subconscious is programmed with a

survival mode and your instincts are trying to keep you safe. (There may be an unknown predator or poisonous berries around the corner!) The unfamiliar is triggering your fear switch. When you know *why* this is happening, it's easier to get a little perspective on *what* is happening.

3. **Take baby steps.** The worst thing you can do is wait for the fear to go away. The only way to make it leave is to step back into your comfort zone, but that's not where you want to be to make the most of this life. If you want to be your best self, then from time to time you must stretch yourself and do things differently. Perhaps it's time to let go of an old belief, improve your health or set a new boundary. Whatever you're trying to accomplish, think of one small step you can take today. Maybe a new route to work to signal your brain that it needs to be open to change. Call a friend and ask for support. Or look up a new recipe to cook a healthy meal or make a breakfast smoothie. Try one of the quick fixes in Chapter 6.

When you are stuck in fear there is no flow. You are at a standstill. Once you get moving again, things will start to fall into place. Like a car standing still, it's much harder to change direction than when the vehicle is in motion.

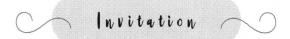

Invitation

Which statement stood out most for you? I recommend you become more conscious of when that belief or fear is triggered so you can start the process of letting it go.

If fears come up—now or in the future—remember my three tips to deal with fear: Expect, Accept, and take a Baby Step.

CHAPTER 15

Unconscious Self-Medication

Following the wake-up call at my naturopath when I found out I had hypoglycemia, I started the strict no sugar, white flour, or yeast diet. A few days after starting my new health regimen, my husband-at-the-time left for the US for a business trip. When he came home, he looked at me and told me my eyes were different. I no longer had this addicted look. *Not what you want to hear when your husband returns after two weeks....*

It was true. Though I never realized it.

I had been self-medicating. It was not obvious because I worked as a product manager in charge of chocolate at an international cookie company. A variety of chocolates sat on on my desk at all times. We were either testing new recipes, creating new products, or tasting the latest introduction from our competitors. All my colleagues ate a lot of chocolate and cookies as well, so there was no reason to consider my consumption abnormal.

Over the years, I learned that a lot of people are self-medicating. They respond to a need of their body and unconsciously give it what it needs. In my case, I had to eat a lot of sugar to use the insulin my body was producing at a too-high rate in order to avoid a hypoglycemic crash. The sugar was a temporary solution, designed to get my body through the existing flare in insulin. If I had been aware of the problem I could have taken a step back to see the bigger picture, but as it was, I was unconsciously putting out fires. My body helped me steer clear from a hypoglycemic episode most of the time—sacrificing long-term health for short-term survival.

The side effect was a never-ending spiral of continuous insulin production. When I was made aware of this mechanism and followed the advice of my naturopath to stop eating sugar cold turkey, he warned me I might get sick and feel like I had the flu. I did. But I stuck it out.

Most people are not aware they are self-medicating. Especially when they support themselves with something seemingly "normal." Things like sugar, alcohol, intense exercise, overworking, over sexing.

They, like me, were not aware this only solves the problem short-term. The body is trying to survive and balances adrenaline and hormone levels with whatever it can stimulate you to eat or do. Because if you do not get through today there is no reason to worry about next month or next year.

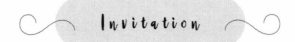

Invitation

Is there a possibility you might be self-medicating? Did you recognize any of the examples? If so, you might want to dive into your health.

If your regular physician cannot find anything wrong with you although you do not feel well, it might be worth contacting a naturopath or the like.

> For eight years traditional doctors were unable to figure out why I was tired a lot of the time. No matter how many tests they did. I was fortunate to be guided to a naturopath who immediately recognized my hypoglycemia.

Are You Numbing Your Pain?

The disbalance can be physical, emotional, or energetic. We are very smart creatures and we intuitively find a way to avoid what we cannot face or handle.

Very few people love and accept themselves completely. It's something I'm still working on.

> **TRUTH**: If something is not present inside you, you cannot find it outside of you. Not for long and not for real.

Lack of self-love or emotional pain can result in many depriving patterns. Whether you are filling yourself up with food, satisfying that hole inside with your drug of choice, or choosing to engage in meaningless sex, mindless shopping, or excessive gaming. Whether you turn to your work and fill your days with to-do lists or whether you start taking care of everyone else but yourself. There are so many varieties of how people deal with a lack of self-love or other form of emotional pain that the list is endless.

The tricky thing is that a lot of these coping mechanisms can be disguised as actually doing something good. Working hard or taking on too much responsibility can look really positive, on the surface. Once you start delving deeper you will see that it is only a way to keep yourself busy, to fill your calendar up so that you do not have the time or the energy left to worry about what you are really doing in your life. If you numb yourself with your drug or habit of choice, you will not have to feel the pain you have inside you.

Emotional eating is a sign of this as well. Rather than going out of their mind because they cannot handle their emotions, people numb their feelings by stuffing them away.

You can dissociate yourself from your life and what is going on by placing something between you and your feelings. As long as you feel anything but the pain. You can only feel one emotion at a time so when you are excited about the gaming, the food, the whatever, you cannot feel sad or alone or not worthy.

Now before you go and think, *Oh Iris, but that's not me,* I would like you to take a moment and be honest with yourself. Is this really not you?

Do not make the mistake of believing the people who numb their feelings through self-medication are a raving mad mess. Most of them are highly functional. They may allow themselves to experience certain feelings, but stay away from specific memories or triggers.

Chances are, you are very sophisticated in how you avoid the pain. Perhaps you are so smart in dealing with this that on the surface it looks like you have it all together. People might envy you for your perfect life.

I truly believe most of us find it difficult to fully love ourselves. To accept and appreciate every single bit of who we are and of what we have done.

All too often we skip over the hard parts or darker bits and make ourselves believe we are all right. That it's okay. But it's not. Every time you deny who you truly are; every time you make excuses for yourself or someone else; every time you hold back, you die a little more inside.

I know I still do not love myself fully. It's a work in progress. I love and appreciate myself so much more than several years ago, but there is still room for growth. That's all right. As long as I am aware of that and alert to where I get myself stuck.

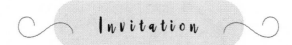

Invitation

What is your vice? What is your go-to thing to feel better or to hide? It might be harmless. It may be innocent. But on the off-chance that you are self-medicating or numbing your pain, I think it is worth asking yourself the question.

As I said, the disbalance can be physical, emotional, or energetic. Or even a combination. The question is not what you did wrong, but what you can shift so you can take better care of yourself and feel better as a result!

Reading this book might give you an idea of what your coping mechanism is. Make sure to reach out for support from someone who is an expert on whatever area you need help with. There is no need to suffer or struggle on your own, not in any area of your life.

To get clear on where you get yourself stuck I invite you to do the following: set an alarm on your phone or computer twice per day for the coming week. Pick times when you most likely have a few minutes to yourself, for example your lunch break and before you go to bed. At these times, take a moment to ground yourself: place your feet firmly on the floor and ask yourself the following questions:

Did I numb my pain today?

How did I do that?

Make sure that you let the answer bubble up from inside you. Do not try to make anything happen. Try not to judge yourself.

By bringing your own awareness to the possibility that you might be numbing your pain, you take an important step. Allow yourself to get clear on where you do this and the stories you are telling yourself. You can start shifting things from there.

CHAPTER 16

The Myth of Going it Alone

Usually we think doing something by ourselves is better. Perhaps not consciously, but we often have an ingrained belief that our achievement is worth more when done on our own, or an accomplishment is more precious when we worked hard for it. Interesting, right?

The Need for Control

Humans try to keep themselves safe by taking control of everything they can. When you do take control over your experience, you feel that you then control the result. You think you do—but you don't.

All you do is exhaust yourself. You limit your possibilities and squander a large part of the time and energy you have over things you can't control, though not for lack of trying.

You might say, "That's not true. I've done this and that and it yielded a result."

Sure. I'm not claiming you don't have the capacity to create. In fact, I would claim you have EVERY capacity to create. Just not how you think.

You think you create by doing, but in truth you create by attracting—by being.

> **TRUTH**: You create by allowing things to take shape in your experience, not by willing them into being through action.

Remember what I said about 80% of results stemming from the energy? You think you can control not only the manifestation process but the things that may hurt you, and you try to keep them out by over-controlling things. You try to keep a tight leash on everything you experience. Some of you package it nicely and make it sound like you are actually opening up and are allowing things into your experience.

And you do, from time to time.

Except it feels more like accidental mistakes when your control slips and you can't prevent that manifestation from coming in, rather than it resulting from a conscious and deliberate allowing of that vibration.

You feel hurt. You're scared and afraid and in order for you to feel like you have a modicum of control over your experience, you exert control in all the things you can get your hands on.

You even try to control other people. And when you can't, you try to control what you think they were thinking and accept "worrying about what other people might think" as your experience.

You can't win if you play not to lose.

You can't win if you're strapped up so tightly that the energy can't flow freely.

You can't win if you exhaust yourself and your body by keeping too many plates spinning.

In order to win, you need to understand the rules of the game. And the rules are not what you made them to be but what was installed when the original game was created. The game of humans here on Earth. The game of creation.

The goal is to have a human experience. The goal is not to screw yourself up and hold on tight in an attempt to have any negative emotions pass you by.

The goal is not walling yourself in and closing yourself off from this human experience by keeping other people out.

The goal is not trying to go this alone for fear of pain of refusal, for fear of not being accepted or worthy or loved.

All these fears do is keep you in a negative spiral. And though no doubt that itself is a very human experience, that is not what you came here to do.

You came here to savor the delight of all the aspects of human life, of all the possibilities laid out in front of you.

So I ask you to open up. To let other people and experiences in. To allow yourself to peek from behind your walls and then find out you will not need them at all.

As long as you focus on the experience of being human, on the joys of accepting that your duty is not to do it all by yourself, but to enjoy and delight in the rays of being this wonderful creature. This unlimited store of potential. To know you can create anything you can conceive of, including the bad stuff.

Lift your head up high and set your sights on what you *want* to achieve and experience. On what you *want* to receive.

Accepting Help

I like doing things myself. I honestly suck at delegating. That's not to say I will not let anyone do anything—but only if I know they excel at it. Like my editor. I completely trust her expertise and experience and I could not do this without her. But if the task at hand is something I am good at, I'm often tempted to do it myself. That's so much easier. At least then I know it's done well. It's much faster, too, because I don't have to explain anything to anyone and then check later whether they did a decent job.

I'm pretty perfectionistic and have a great eye for detail. Those character traits make it hard for me to hand over the reins. Besides, I like control.

Except…I have learned how it limits me. Sure, the first time you delegate something it takes more time, and perhaps even the second and third time, but then the bliss begins! You can now focus your awareness on other things (like reading a book in the sun!) while your assistant takes care of handling those emails. This may sound completely logical, but the truth is many people think something is more valuable if they did it without help.

Even more so, they believe their productivity is a measure of how well they did on any given day. For many years, a good day for me was a day when I got a lot done. There is nothing wrong with being productive, but it should not determine how good you feel about yourself. Some days are slower days, some days are integration days, some days you are sick. We need rest, as I think we have established by now. However, we tend not to value the rest; only the tangible results.

You are not meant to do this alone. You are not earning brownie points for draining yourself by doing too much or by doing it all alone. Pushing through does not make you a better person; it only makes you exhausted.

Ask for Support

When we are overwhelmed or made a mistake we tend to buckle down and pour even more time and effort into working our way to the surface or fixing the problem at hand. We close ourselves off, often feeling ashamed or inadequate. Because everyone else seems to be living a picture-perfect life without breaking a sweat. News-flash: they are struggling as much as you are. They simply don't share it on social media—people curate their feed! Sure, they may be great at things you can't do and vice versa. But I can promise you they are working just as hard to be liked and juggling all the elements of their own lives.

Talk about it. Share your struggles with someone you trust, someone who can relate (because if someone doesn't understand your situation you will only feel misunderstood). When you are self-employed, speak to a fellow entrepreneur. When you are a mom, speak to another mother about toddler challenges and balancing the different hats.

When you share your fears and concerns, you open up to the flow. Speak from the heart. I don't mean have a venting session to complain about everything and everyone where you both get to conclude life is miserable. Though that might feel pleasant in the moment, it will only drain you further. I mean share with the intention of connecting to one another, to invite in the light, to understand, perhaps to laugh about things that went wrong. Give other people a chance to support you, emotionally or practically. You do not have to fight this battle all on your own. I trust you would prefer that your friends reach out for support rather than struggle silently, right?

> **TRUTH**: Asking for support is a sign of strength, not weakness.

We are in this together and others have something valuable to offer as well. We must give them the chance to do so.

Know that you can ask for help from both the seen and the unseen dimensions. Turn to whichever greater power you believe in. I've seen help arrive in the most unexpected ways: a stranger stepping up to pay for your groceries when you forgot your wallet; a surprise bouquet of roses dropped off by a friend who knows you're having a hard time; the reassurance of a song on the radio singing exactly what you needed to hear.

Do not forget to ask your angels, spirit guides, and teachers for help as well! They are waiting for you to reach out and request support because they will never interfere with your free will. You can ask them for what you need by saying it aloud or in your mind—or even write it down. When I make a request, I like to add "for the highest good of all concerned," trusting that sometimes things happen for a reason that is not yet clear. Once you solicit your guides' support, they work their magic in powerful ways.

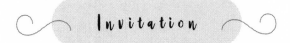

Invitation

What do you need help with right now? Take a moment to answer this question honestly. If your answer is "nothing," think again. Unless you have fully outsourced the majority of things in your life, chances are you can use a helping hand. Whether that is a cleaning lady or a window washer, feedback on an idea, hiring specific expertise or a listening ear. I invite you to think of at least one thing you can ask for support with this week.

The solution does not have to cost money. Chances are you know more people than you realize. Asking a friend to think about where to find the right support can be a great way to start.

CHAPTER 17

The Illusion of "No Time for Breaks"

When I was writing my novel *Poisoned Arrow* I had to stay super alert on my own self-care regimen. I admit at times it was tempting to push through and skip breaks (or even meals).

As the deadline approached, I'd worked on my novel the entire Saturday and I was fully committed to keep going the next day. I was going to finish my manuscript on time!

Until I remembered one of the "rules" I tell all my clients—and almost forgot to apply for myself. Which is to take breaks.

Because that's how it happens. When your to-do list sneaks up on you and urges you on. When you feel like there's only so much time to accomplish all that you need to get done. Or when there's a clear deadline.

None of that matters.

Seriously. Because if you don't take good care of yourself, your productivity and creativity go down the drain. You lose focus and even though you're busy all the time, it isn't all that effective. I know.

Even research knows this.

It's been shown time and again that the brain (and the body) need time off to function better.

There's a reason Monday is my most productive day by far, hands down, no exception. Because I always take the weekend off. Or at least one day. Like that Sunday.

Though I almost didn't.

TRUTH: We need twenty-four hours of blissful "everything but work" so the brain can get to a deeper level of relaxation.

No checking your email, not even for just five minutes. Because you'll be thinking about what you read and crafting responses in your mind. Just don't.

Do yourself a favor and take the day off. Especially if you have a lot to do. Your body and your work will thank you for it.

I spent that Sunday reading in the sun. What will you do?

Make it Part of Your Schedule

If you want to be more productive you need to start doing less, not more! Pushing through does not mean you will get more done. You need breaks, you need time off, you need to recoup. *Then* you will be fresh, your mind and body will be reinvigorated, and as a result you will be more productive. With a guaranteed minimum of twenty days off in addition to an average of seven national holidays, the Netherlands is one of the countries with the most days off. We are also one of the most productive countries. That is not a coincidence.

Make sure to plan your breaks. Not just lunch and a not-too-busy weekend. Schedule that one hour for yourself and your time off in the form of long weekends and vacations. Plug those big boulders into your calendar first, especially if you run your own business, but also when you're a stay-at-home mom or do volunteer work. We all need a breather.

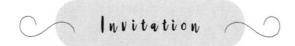

Have a look at your agenda for the coming week. Is there enough room for relaxation and breaks? Have you scheduled time for fresh air and some much-needed vitamin D? What else can you do to support yourself? Think of meals, exercise, oxygen. But also things that recharge and energize you. Is there enough room for connection with loved ones and for fun?

What will you do to take some of the pressure off and treat yourself—and your body—with kindness?

Why You Should Extend Your (Lunch) Break

Your lunch is important. Not just what you are eating, most of you are aware of that, but also how you are eating it.

We are all busy and usually our to-do list is longer than we can get done today. This sense of pressure makes us feel like there is not enough time and before you know it you're having lunch behind your desk or standing at the kitchen counter, barely tasting what you're eating. Perhaps you skip your lunch break altogether, or quickly wolf down a snack as you're running to your next meeting or to pick up the kids. Because you are so busy, there's no time left to waste on eating lunch. Right?

Think again. Taking a proper lunch break will save you time!

Research has shown that taking even a short twenty-minute break helps increase your concentration and your energy level.

It also has a positive effect on your productivity and creativity. Several years ago, I remember reading about research which concluded that people who took a forty-five-minute lunch break were more productive than those who continued working and ate behind their desk.

While you think you are saving time by not having a lunch break, you are actually slowing down your productivity so much that your friend who went for lunch and perhaps a quick walk will still get more done during that day.

Skipping breaks reduces your creativity, too. Your brain needs time off in order to make the connections needed for that aha! moment. When I studied creative thinking techniques, I loved hearing about the four Bs: Bed, Bath, Bus and Forest (which in Dutch starts with a B, too.) In these places, your mind can wander because you are usually not focused on work or coming up with solutions. These moments give incubation time for creative answers.

> **TRUTH**: One of the fastest methods to stimulate innovation and flow is to turn your focus away from the problem you are trying to solve. Distract yourself and give your brain a break.

Those are plenty of reasons to allow yourself a decent lunch break. Food is not only nutrition for your body; it improves your mood, too. When a meal is prepared with love, I believe you can feel and taste it. On those occasions, food nourishes not just the body but your spirit as well.

As a spiritual being, we cannot expect to do what we came here to do while neglecting the vehicle we have been given (our body), nor skimp on the nourishment of our soul.

Therefore, I recommend you incorporate a healthy lunch break into your day. It's good for your body, your mind, and your soul. For your job or family too.

Don't just take a decent break on days when you have plenty of time, but also (especially!) on days where your to-do list seems endless and dictates the pace of the day. After all is said and done, you'll be glad you took the time to recharge.

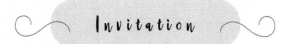

Invitation

When you look back at this week, this month—how many times did you take a lunch break away from your desk, focusing fully on something not related to your work or to-do list?

Be honest: how much time you are taking for your lunch break. If it's less than thirty minutes, try changing your schedule to incorporate at least a half hour for lunch. If you already take that much time to eat during the day, you might want to add a (short) walk outside. Already doing that too? High five!

Sleep Your Way to the Top

You can sleep your way to the top. Though it's not what you may think. I mean literally, by having more SLEEP.

I knew sleep was important, but I was still surprised how much a lack of shut-eye impacts our productivity, creativity, and the quality of our work—and life.

According to *Harvard Business Review*, there is a proven link between effective leadership and getting enough sleep.

"Sleep deprivation impairs the ability to focus attention selectively: Research shows that after roughly 17 to 19 hours of wakefulness (say, at 11 PM or 1 AM for someone who got up at 6 AM), individual performance on a range of tasks is equivalent to that of a person with a blood alcohol level of 0.05%. That's the legal drinking limit in many countries. After roughly 20 hours of wakefulness (2 AM), this same person's performance equals that of someone with a blood alcohol level of 0.1%, which meets the legal definition of drunk in the United States."
—Van Dam and Van der Helm, 2016.

You may have heard—or experienced—that a lack of sleep deteriorates your visual and motor skills. What may be less familiar is that sleep deprivation has an even bigger effect on higher-order mental skills such as problem solving, reasoning, organizing, and executing plans.

Next time you consider sending that late-night email, you may want to wait until morning because a good night's sleep not only ensures you are fresh and focused, but often leads to new insights.

Do you want to avoid tunnel vision and improve decision-making? Guess what? Sleep more!

Want to get better at creative problem solving? Take a nap, you will be twice as likely to solve the problem than when you stay awake. The list goes on.

More sleep is one of the easiest—and most relaxing—ways to increase productivity and perform to the best of your ability. And it is not something that impacts you alone.

"In a sleep-deprived state, your brain is more likely to misinterpret cues and overreact to emotional events, and you tend to express your feelings in a more negative manner and tone of voice. Recent studies have shown that people who have not had enough sleep

are less likely to fully trust someone else. Another experiment has demonstrated that employees feel less engaged with their work when their leaders have had a bad night of sleep."
—Van Dam and Van der Helm, 2016.

I'm sure the same applies to your engagement with your kids or partner when you had little sleep. Now everybody gets cranky.

Obviously lack of trust is not ideal when you are building a team or forging a new relationship.

Another reason to get more sleep is that it prevents burnout. A lack of sleep leads to experiencing more stress which, in turn, reduces the quality of your sleep. A never-ending story.

Evidently there are many other negative effects of poor sleep on your health. Plenty of reasons to turn in early tonight. I know this is easier said than done and often requires a change in both (corporate) culture and personal behavior. But it all starts with awareness.

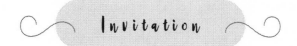

Invitation

Are you getting enough sleep? If not, what is the reason? Are you simply going to bed too late or do you have trouble sleeping? When your mind is too busy and your thoughts are running a mile a minute, try grounding before going to bed. Avoid watching TV at least one hour before bedtime and refrain from working on your computer or tablet after dinner. Consider a walk, a bath, reading, or meditating instead.

When you are going through an emotionally challenging time, make sure you have someone to talk to. If needed, seek professional support in the form of a coach, mentor or specialist. Sending you a big hug!

A private client realized how much better she felt when she slept for eight hours. I helped her with the mindset shift needed to prioritize going to bed early, and the extra hours of sleep worked wonders for her.

Make sure to air your bedroom daily as oxygen improves the quality of your sleep. Most mattresses need replacing after several years. Something to keep in mind if you are not sleeping well.

CHAPTER 18

The Danger of Pushing Through

Pushing through is not a healthy practice. You are putting a strain on your body. I'm not talking about the occasional late night, whether it's to meet a deadline or enjoy a party. That's part of life and we are not here to be monks. But a continuous strain erodes your health.

When to Push Through and When to Surrender

I know all about pushing through. There were days (years!) when I was the queen of pushing through. I didn't stop. I kept going until I literally had nothing left to give.

I had burned myself out by giving so much of myself to everyone and everything around me.

I felt responsible. Responsible for doing a good job—even when my boss was transferred and I had to do her job, too.

Responsible for being a good "housewife," even when I worked full-time and had a long, traffic-filled commute.

Responsible for my partner and his family's well-being because his father had passed away, as if his death wasn't allowed to impact me—thinking I had to be the strong one.

Responsible for being perfect and doing everything perfectly.

I gave and gave until only adrenaline kept me going. Not that I noticed…I was too busy pushing through.

Pushing through has taught me there is an end to what I can do, an end to what I am responsible for, and an end to how perfect something (or someone!) has to be.

It also showed me I can do a lot if it's really needed. That my willpower is a strength I can muster in case of emergencies.

Surrender. Now that is an entirely different energy, much more subtle and infinitely more powerful. It requires a special approach.

Surrender is about letting go. About trust. About letting someone else (the Universe, spirit, God, Buddha—whichever term works for you) take the wheel.

It's about releasing control and allowing yourself to be taken to where you need to go.

It's about believing the Universe knows better than you.

Surrender is scary. Where pushing through is about taking the wheel, surrender is about sitting in the backseat—with a blindfold on.

Surrender is hard. While pushing through might seem hard (and is a lot of work), surrender is much harder.

People often ask me how to surrender, and I wish there was a magic button we could push to make that happen.

As it is, surrender is about taking small steps. It's about deciding to stop pushing through. It's about releasing control. It's about letting go of attachment to the outcome. It's about accepting you don't know how or when you'll get there. If you'll even get there.

Surrender is the most important thing you'll ever do—one of the hardest things, but infinitely powerful.

When you surrender you open up to the Universe and the beauty of life.

When you surrender you admit you don't know.

When you surrender you open your heart and your mind and your life to miracles.

You allow yourself to be taken to where you're guided; to where you're meant to be.

Surrender is powerful and beautiful and messy. I don't think I've ever surrendered fully without crying. Crying helps me release and let go.

The tears help me see I've come to the end of my rope, that this isn't working. And though I've tried to do things my way, though I've given it a lot of effort, willpower isn't what is going to get me where I want to go.

So I SURRENDER.

That's what I wish for you, too.

Here's to surrender, one moment at a time.

And when you realize you've taken back control (because for most of us it's so automatic), all you have to do is take a deep breath, relax your shoulders, and decide to surrender again. And again.

If you have kids waking you up at night, that's an even bigger reason to take good care of yourself. Because when you get grumpy and exhausted, guess who becomes moody and hard to handle? Exactly: your children.

When it is hard to shift from doing to being, this guided activation will help you be more present and more in touch with what is going on around you. Listen to Release What No Longer Serves You on **www.radianttools.nl**.

Are You Stuck in Overdrive?

In a session with a client I was reminded of the difference between SWEET POWER™ and willpower. And how that is tied immediately to our energy and which battery we use.

When you are operating on willpower—which for most people is the majority of the time—you are using adrenaline as your major power source. This means something has triggered you into being alert. This could be a deadline at work, worry about something or someone, emotional stress, or, more recently, a pandemic.

There's a reason doctors are sounding the alarm bell because a disconcerting number of people are about to be burned out. According to *Forbes*, 52% of survey respondents across demographic categories were suffering from burnout in 2021—20% higher than pre-pandemic in the US (Kelly 2021).

It's not a problem that our body responds with adrenaline to save us from (perceived) danger. The problem lies in never shutting off.

> **TRUTH**: We have become so used to living on adrenaline and counting on it to get us through the day that we deplete ourselves—physically, emotionally, mentally and energetically.

Our body believes we are in danger, so it prioritizes creating adrenaline over everything else! If you are running from a mountain lion, having the adrenaline to escape or hide is much more important than things like regeneration of cells or proper digestion.

However, if your body never gets the "all clear" signal then it never knows it is safe. It never knows it's okay to start prioritizing normal and crucial body processes and to stop the production of adrenaline above all else.

I have lived most of my life on willpower and it took many years, a burnout, and tough decisions to get to a place where I can live from flow. Rather than muscling through, I choose to pause and listen to my body. To make sure I am not stuck in overdrive.

Willpower and adrenaline can give you that extra boost when you need it. Using it as your main source of (false) energy ensures you will not only empty your tank, but likely destroy part of the engine in the process.

Chances are you will not only empty what you had, but you will carve a hole and burrow down deep—doing damage to yourself and your physical body. I have done that and I know how sneaky this process can be. You might think you know where to stop and when to pause, but when your system is running on adrenaline, it's very hard to notice you are using emergency energy rather than your normal supply. If you go at it too long, some of the damage might be irreparable. For many people, a weak spot will always remain in their bodies.

Save your adrenaline for emergencies. And remember to shift back from willpower to SWEET POWER™ in time. Your body will thank you for it. You will notice you have more energy, in a more sustainable way.

If you are not sure whether you are operating on adrenaline, ask yourself whether you are present in your head or aware of your body.

> **TIP:** If you have to think about the answer, you are in your head.

To shift, I advise you to pause. Take a moment to relax—truly relax. Sitting down while mentally ticking things off your to-do list does not count.

We need your system to slow down. This is a great moment to ground yourself, and breathe consciously. Make your exhale longer than your inhale.

The only "problem" is that once you take a break and your body understands it is safe—because we are no longer running around trying to get away from that lion—your adrenaline production will stop. And you will feel tired as a result.

This is crucial: it *seems* you were not tired before, but that is only because your adrenaline stopped you from being able to feel how drained you actually were!

That is how you get burned out and damage your body. You are not aware of how exhausted you are because you keep going.

Now that it is safe to relax and recharge, your body recognizes this as an opportunity to refill the energetic stock and to catch up on some vital processes, such as regenerating cells. It finally has the time and safe space (and energy).

Make sense?

Keep your adrenaline supply for emergencies only: mountain lions, deadlines, or otherwise. Live the rest of your life on healthy energy. The one that does not deplete and damage your entire system.

Remember: the difference between willpower and SWEET POWER™ is easy to feel.

When things feel forced and driven, when it is hard to sit still and you are operating from your mind, chances are you are using willpower and are banking on adrenaline. You are pushing through.

With SWEET POWER™ you will feel a sense of flow, an inner calm, a trust and knowing that even when things do not go according to plan, you will be okay.

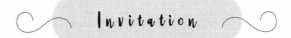

Invitation

Take a break, slow down, ground. Get out of your head and into your body. Do something physical, but avoid activities like running or watching a scary movie or a sports event that will stimulate adrenaline production. Do some yoga, tai chi, or light stretching. Take a walk, bask in the sun, get a massage, or take a salt bath. Or do something creative you enjoy, whether it's painting, pottery, knitting, or baking. You can even massage your own feet. As long as you do something fun that helps you relax.

CHAPTER 19

The Effect of Your Emotions

Our emotions have a huge effect on our energy level and how we experience our day. When you are in love or exhilarated, you feel like you can take on the world. When you are sad or frustrated, you probably feel drained or heavy. I believe it's important to become more consciously aware of our emotions and know we can choose to shift them—without ignoring the hurt. Because there is something we need to do first.

Lean into the Discomfort

I recently woke up with a feeling of unease. A feeling something was wrong, even though I could not pinpoint what that might be. I sensed an overpowering sense of loss, of something being off.

I remembered to breathe in love and exhale worry. Doing so helped a little, but an underlying feeling of discomfort remained.

We have the tendency to "fix" the discomfort, to not feel off or jumbled.

We want to feel happy, calm and at peace. We want things to work out in our favor. We want to smile and enjoy the good bits of life. That's why we are here, right? To enjoy.

I truly believe it's important to follow your joy—crucial, even.

Why bother to look at discomfort?

Because it has something to tell you. Something wants your attention. You have the opportunity to heal a pain, something that happened in the (recent) past. You are given the chance to release and open up room for more affirming experiences.

Often we miss these healing opportunities because we reach for something—anything—to distract us. We focus on what makes us forget the pain. We go on social media, read a book, listen to a song, or perhaps call a friend.

All the while not realizing we are moving away from what needs our attention.

Lean into the discomfort. Allow yourself to feel the pain so you can move through it and let it out of your system.

I know how daunting that can be. I've had moments where the pain seemed insurmountable. But a good cry is so much more effective than running away from the ache. When you allow yourself to fully feel the pain, anger, fear, or sadness—rather than suppress it so it's continuously present in the background—you will be able to release the emotion and stop carrying that energy with you. Stop lugging it around like a heavy backpack you can never set down because it's tied to you.

∽ EXERCISE ∽

Gift yourself a moment of stillness, of being present with what you feel. Whether it makes you happy or sad. Allow the feeling of worry or dread to intensify. Lean into it. Let it fill you up, and go from there.

In my experience, it rarely takes longer than a few minutes when you completely allow the emotion to surface.

I believe it's important to accept and acknowledge what you feel. That it's essential to living a happy and fulfilling life. Paramount if you want to be true to who you are.

Being fully yourself means allowing the "bad" to be present as much as the good. Because the sooner you allow yourself to feel the unease, the faster you can move through it. Not because it's something you need to get over quickly, but because it allows you to focus on the next thing you are meant to do or experience.

Be true to you. Your body and soul will thank you for it. Suppressing emotions and feelings consumes part of your energy, and it only tips you off-balance further.

I asked: "What does this unease want to tell me?"

The answer: "You should relax more. You are still trying to do too much. Allow yourself to BE more. Be present, fully present, with all your awareness. Be available to the urges that move you, that move through you."

Like I said earlier, we often teach what we have to learn ourselves.

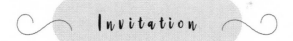

Invitation

The next time you feel unsettled, sad, or off, take a moment to stand still and lean into the discomfort. Allow it to intensify. Cry if needed and ask yourself, *What does this feeling want to tell me? What needs my attention?* Then trust the answer to bubble up. Whether it is then and there or later in the form of a sign or something that stands out in a conversation, a song on the radio, or whatnot. Trust and you will get your answer. Trust that you will get clarity on which insights want to come through or what needs to be released.

I remember calling a friend at 11:00 p.m. because I couldn't stop crying. I scared her to pieces because I couldn't even speak. She feared someone had died. That was not the case, but that *was* what it felt like. As a sensitive soul, I sometimes feel too much. After seeing *Titanic* I was shattered. I've not been able to watch that movie since. I avoid violent films or books. They just make me feel miserable.

A client who loved noir movies noticed her preference shift as she worked with me. The more she became aware of her sensitivity and in touch with herself, the less appeal those films had to her.

Do not worry if your fondness for something changes. It's an indication of growth.

We Store Emotions in Our Body

There is also an energetic component to how not expressing emotions impacts us.

The energy flowing in and out of every human being is equal. The differences arise in the way the human body is ready and able to cope with the amount of energy that flows into it. Many patterns and habits have formed little scar tissues on the cells open to receive this energy. When the space in the cell is occupied by emotions, toxins, or heavy metals, there is less room for the energy to enter the cell.

A space can only be occupied with one thing (matter) at the same time in the same dimension of time and space. As many people have emotions stored in their human body, there is less room for the energy to move freely. To open up this room again, the emotion can be released in several ways. For example, share the story with a loved one who is listening with their heart and soul open. Or release the energy during a healing session. This is something I often support my clients with.

When someone shares an emotional or traumatic experience it's important to hold space, giving them your full focus and awareness.

Try to postpone judgment; avoid coming up with solutions. Remember, their energy needs to be released and this might be one of the first times they share their story. Even a seemingly small event can have a huge impact if it triggers old pain.

The ability with which humans are able to let go of emotions dictates the room available for their energy to flow freely. When some people are "stuck," they are caught in this cycle of reliving or not releasing the event or emotions. This not only takes up a lot of energy, but also allows the incoming energy minimum space. Which could end in a vicious circle.

These insights fascinate me. To me it's clear how we can get clogged over time, by repressing emotions for a variety of reasons. Often it feels easier to hide our tears for fear of being seen as weak or emotional. It's essential to realize that suppressing your emotions goes further than just that moment and might be something you carry with you for a long time. I believe it's one of the things that dim your light.

In addition to this, I believe that when you store emotions in your body, those cells are not able to perform their normal duties. Because part of the cell is used as a storage facility, thus unable to function to its full capacity. Disease may start to develop as a result.

The energy of the emotions has to go somewhere. You can either express it (explode) or hold it in (implode). This goes for both positive and negative emotions. Holding in happiness is not healthy, either.

> **TIP**: Stop swallowing your emotions. Your physical, emotional, and energetic well-being will benefit.

Accept Where You Are

Life is about riding the ups and downs. The ups are fun, gliding on high. It's the downs we need to learn to navigate. To not be pulled under by a current deeper than we can reach. To not keep looking through a dark lens, but take a step away for some perspective.

Life can hit us hard, and usually unexpectedly. Living can be fabulously beautiful as well. It's tempting to numb what you feel so the downs are not as low, but it means you erase some of those delightful highs.

> **TRUTH:** Many people are not fully grounded, not just because they work too much with their head, but just as often to escape their body and not feel as much.

Life is about balance. We know the dualities of light and dark, up and down, are what make this such a crazy good adventure.

How do we navigate those depths? What can you do to pull yourself out of a rut and feel better—without pretending the "bad" stuff is not there?

This is not about ignoring what happens or suppressing what you feel. This is about accepting what is, and moving on from there.

I'm single and I have been for years. I know my guy is out there and we'll meet at the right time. For a while I used that as a shield—not consciously of course. Trusting that he's out there made me attach more to that future vision than to be aware of the present moment.

I'm good at being alone. As a sensitive soul, I need time for myself.

When I'm not reading a book or spending time with family and friends, there's plenty to do. I always have more ideas than I have time. So I kind of skipped over the fact I'm alone.

I AM SINGLE.

And that's fine. But for quite some time it was something I didn't want to look at. Being single made me feel I had done something wrong. I've done lots of inner work on this topic. Somehow that made me feel that was enough. I'd done the work, right?

Except there's one thing I forgot: to accept it.

You might have something in your personal or professional life that is not how you would want it to be. It's time to look it in the face, to acknowledge that this is true—no matter how much you wish it wasn't.

To get out of that valley of not having or grieving or missing, you need to accept that this is where you are now, for this moment. Only then can you start to climb out of the valley toward neutral... and then up high.

Invitation

What in your life have you avoided staring straight in the face? What is something, perhaps seemingly small, you resist looking at?

Write it down, look at it, and let yourself feel what this is like. If tears come, let them surface. If you are angry or tired or disappointed, if you feel betrayed by life or the Universe, voice it. Say it out loud, write it in your journal, jump up and down—whatever it is that helps you look at and experience the void.

Cry all you want, take a walk or a salt bath. Soothe yourself once you have stared it in the eye. Once you are able to fully accept it and say, *Yes, this is part of my life right now. It might suck, but here it is.*

Then take a deep breath and release. You can let it go. Ask for the next best step and trust it will be shown to you. Because you are not meant to stay down here.

> Life is always in motion, swinging back and forth. And the time
> has come for your pendulum to start swinging again.
>
> Out of the void.

Three Common Mistakes to Avoid Pain

We've all been hurt over time and we all found a way to deal with the emotional pain. We also came up with a strategy to avoid future pain. I've done it myself. I see it in clients and in the people around me.

**These are the three most common ways
to prevent pain (or so we think):**

1. We leave our body.
2. We close our heart.
3. We hide in our head.

Biggest Mistake #1 – We Leave Our Body

Now hold on before you think that's not you. *There is a 95% chance that you do this, too!*

Let me explain what I mean by leaving your body.

We are a spiritual being in a human body, and in a normal situation our energetic body is aligned with our physical body. Picture two circles: one is your energetic body and the other is your physical body. In a healthy situation they overlap perfectly so it looks like one circle.

When you are in pain (or trying to avoid being hurt), your energetic body withdraws from your physical body. Imagine the energetic circle moving upwards so the bottom half hovers around your shoulders. Now your physical and energetic body overlap less than 50%. Rather than one circle it's more like a figure eight.

It *seems* to do the trick. You feel less (because you are literally less present), so it is less painful.

BUT. And this is a big but. Though you seem to have achieved your goal (to avoid pain) you are not actually avoiding it. The pain is still there—less prominent, I'll give you that—but this is not a solution. It's a Band-Aid!

A Band-Aid with the side-effect of being less in touch with your body and what it needs. This is how burnout happens or (chronic) disease develops. We miss all the signals from our body because we chose to be less present.

Make sense?

Unfortunately, that's not our only strategy to deal with (or avoid) heartache and distress.

Biggest Mistake #2 – We Close Our Heart

In an attempt to preempt the pain, we disconnect. Have you ever broken up with someone because you did not want them to do it? Or closed the virtual door on a person because of the turmoil that got stirred up inside you?

We do this in platonic relationships as well (think family, friends, colleagues). We close ourselves off. If you are the first to close your heart, then it's less painful when you are disappointed. Alas, this comes with a huge undesired side-effect as well.

When you close your heart, you shut down a part of your life-force energy. That is the energy you need to function and be vibrantly alive.

When someone loses the twinkle in their eyes or is lower in energy, that is a telltale sign their heart chakra is not fully open.

Closing your heart will literally lower the amount of energy you have. It's a very common way for most of us to deal with pain and (potential) disappointment.

Biggest Mistake #3 – We Hide in Our Head

This is something we do out of habit. We try to control everything, because we think when we are in control of our actions it means we control the outcome. Sadly, that is not the case (as you have probably noticed a couple of times during your life).

Because we cannot control what another person will or will not do, we take preemptive action: we retreat to our head. Whatever part of our consciousness is left, most of our awareness is already halfway back to our home planet.

This tactic, although it can temporarily lessen the pain, comes with a big fat side effect. When you are holing up in your head, you cut off the connection to your intuition. When you lose touch with your intuition, you let go of your most valuable compass. That's a big loss, and most people are not aware that this is the result of their habit.

Three tips to Open Your Heart

The mistakes mentioned in the previous section make clear that in an attempt to minimize pain we have taught ourselves some strategies. Sadly, these strategies all come at a big cost (and none of them deal with the true problem, anyway). Now we need to change these habits. And that's where these tips come into play.

Main Tip #1 – Get Present

Remember the biggest mistake #1? We leave our body. The solution is to be present by returning to our body.

GROUND. It's one of my favorite tools for a reason. Grounding is the fastest and best way to sync your energetic body with your physical body. It allows you to be present and that's the foundation for so much more. I recorded a special short grounding exercise for you to help you be more present so it's easier to open your heart. Listen to it here: **www.radianttools.nl**.

Main Tip #2 - Open Your Heart

Remember the biggest mistake #2? We close our heart. The answer to that is pretty obvious, but unfortunately it's not easy to do. We are so used to keeping our heart closed that it's difficult—and may even feel unnatural—to open it. Remember, this is one of our survival strategies so the pattern is often deeply ingrained.

It's important that you get into the habit of opening your heart, again and again, because this is tied directly to your life-force energy. A closed heart impacts your energy level and well-being. Rather than command you to open your heart at will (I wish there was a spell for that!) I created a tool to support you. I have recorded a special guided activation to help you open your heart. Listen to Open Your Heart And Allow More Love In at **www.radianttools.nl**. You can practice opening your heart every day. The same goes for this next tip.

Main Tip #3 - Relax (and Have Fun!)

Remember the biggest mistake #3? We hide in our head. When you are stuck in your head, your first step is to ground (see the grounding activation in tip #1).

You are hiding in your head partly out of fear and partly out of a desire to control everything, hoping that then you can also manipulate the outcome.

Remember, subconsciously you are trying to avoid the pain.

In order to get you out of your head, we need to get you into your body (hence the grounding) and then Let Go. Release. Relax. Have fun.

If you are anything like me, chances are you are way too serious much too often. Lighten up and do something solely for your enjoyment. Whether that is read a book, take a walk, watch a movie, call your best friend, or eat an entire box of dark chocolates (no, I didn't say that. I would *never* do that...).

When you are having a good time, you are worrying less and there is more flow naturally.

Will this help solve all your troubles and help you have an open heart forevermore? Nope. But these three tips are a big step forward and the foundation for allowing yourself to keep your heart open and your energy flowing.

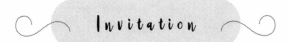

Invitation

I highly recommend you listen to the two activations and have a go at relaxing and having fun. It will make a huge difference in how you feel and how much energy you allow to flow through you. In addition, it will become visible in your appearance. Because you allow more energy to flow through you, you will become more radiant.

CHAPTER 20

The Impact of Your Vibration

Everything is energy—from this book you are reading to the food you ate, even your own thoughts, all have a certain vibrational frequency. This frequency is measurable, thanks to the research of Dr. David R. Hawkins. In the 2004 edition of *Power vs. Force*, he writes about his twenty years of clinical research all across the globe.

His research uses the principle of kinesiology (the study of muscles and their movement, specifically applied to physical conditioning).

Dr. George Goodheart, a pioneer in applied kinesiology, showed "that benign physical stimuli—for instance, beneficial nutritional supplements—would increase the strength of certain indicator muscles, whereas hostile stimuli would cause those muscles to suddenly weaken. The implication was that at a level far below conceptual consciousness, the body "knew," and through muscle testing was able to signal, what was good and bad for it. The classic example...is a universally observed weakening of indicator muscles in the presence of a chemical sweetener; the same muscles strengthen in the presence of a healthful and natural supplement."

Behavioral kinesiology discovered the same principle was true for emotional and intellectual stimuli. Muscle testing is done with your arm held out horizontal—with someone else testing how easy or difficult it is to push your arm down. This is not about physical strength but about pushing just hard enough to test the resistance in the arm. Smiling will strengthen the muscle (your arm will be difficult to push down) while saying "I hate you" will weaken the muscle. When someone's muscle goes weak, there is a temporary break in the electrical system of their nervous system, which results in the muscle responding as if it was momentarily "unplugged". Muscle testing makes the natural break in continuity visible (Weisgerber). I often use muscle testing to check whether a certain food will support my body. As I said before, our body usually knows what is good for us and what is harmful. And this is an easy way to ask that question.

In researching the kinesiological response to truth and falsehood, Hawkins found that a form of collective consciousness seemed to be at work. He used muscle testing to create "a scale of relative truth by which intellectual positions, statements or ideologies could be rated on a range of 1 to 1,000. One can ask, 'This item (book, philosophy, teacher) calibrates at 200 (Y/N?): at 250 (Y/N?),' and so on, until the point of common weak response determines the calibration."

These calibrations collected during his extensive research were used to create a map of the energy fields of human consciousness. The energy of our thoughts—of everything in fact—"exists on a quantifiable spectrum where each point on the spectrum has unique qualities" (Weisberger). Just like a certain radio frequency will lead you to a specific radio station, a certain emotion correlates with a specific vibration. Hawkins' chart illuminates "the scale of consciousness" that ranges from 20 (shame) to 1000 (enlightenment). His research shows, for example, that fear calibrates at 100 whereas love is vibrating at 500. (Hawkins 2004)

If you are wondering what this has to do with your energy level, bear with me.

> "The critical response point in the scale of consciousness calibrates at level 200, which is the level associated with integrity and courage. All attitudes, thoughts, feelings, associations, entities, or historical figures below that level of calibration make a person go weak—those that calibrate higher make subjects go strong. This is the balance point between weak and strong attractors, between negative and positive influence.
>
> At the levels below 200, the primary impetus is personal survival.... As one crosses the demarcation between negative and positive influence into Courage, the well-being of others becomes increasingly important."
> —David R. Hawkins M.D, Ph.D.

The level of 200 on the scale of consciousness is considered the initial level of empowerment. It's characterized by the willingness to stop blaming and accept responsibility for one's own actions, feelings, and beliefs.

TRUTH: Everybody has a base vibration and your experience in life helps you to change and evolve that vibration. Increasing your vibration by even a few points can have a major impact on your physical well-being, your ability to act from love, and your energy level.

In my experience, consciously managing your energy and raising your vibration is one of the fastest ways to create the results you are looking for.

In other words: it's crucial to vibrate above 200 as it makes life so much easier and fun. The more you can raise your vibration, the more you can use your energy to create the life you want.

As I said before: once you shift your energy, *everything* changes.

I have seen many instances where once I was able to shift my energy, the entire situation changed with it. Sometimes miraculously so. Years ago I did a homework exercise from my business coach around purpose. The questions triggered something inside me and before I knew it, I wrote down my mission while bawling my eyes out. Something uncoiled inside me, recognizing the truth of what I was now staring at:

> It is my mission to help raise
> the vibration of the planet so
> more people can live from love.

So much fell into place, while a million questions remained. Ever since, I have been much more conscious about the impact of my vibration. Knowing my mission helped me understand choices I have made throughout my entire life. Like my preference to drink water from a crystal glass. Or hum at my food to raise its vibe. Which doesn't always go unnoticed. I'll never forget my father's face when he asked, "Do you realize you are making noise?" That memory still makes me laugh. It may sound silly, but I can actually feel the difference.

There are many benefits to raising your vibration. Here are the top five.

1. **You will have more energy.** Because you vibrate at a higher level, you have more access to the "power" of your energetic body and thus energy flows in more freely and easily. A higher vibration increases your overall wellbeing as well.

2. **You will be able to feel more love.** As you increase your vibration you let go of lower-level energies such as fear, jealousy, and anger. This opens up room for more love. Love for yourself and love for others. Increased compassion is an important side effect. Something the world, and we, need desperately.

3. **You will be able to hear your inner wisdom better.** As you vibrate at a higher frequency, you become more aligned with your higher self. This alignment makes it easier to hear what your intuition is trying to convey to you.

4. **You will feel more confident.** As you let go of lower-level energies and get more in touch with your true self, you will naturally have more confidence in yourself and what you are here to bring. Even if you are not aware of it, it shows and people will definitely notice.

5. **You will be happier and healthier.** A lot of diseases cannot exist above a certain frequency. The higher your vibration, the healthier you will be. Happiness and health go hand-in-hand.

These benefits demonstrate that the level at which you vibrate impacts many, if not all, areas of your life. Raising your vibration is a continuous process; one you want to stay in touch with and on top of.

There are numerous ways to raise your vibration, such as using essential oils, listening to your favorite music, and dancing. Through the (automatic) process of entrainment—the synchronization of two processes—you can raise your vibe by being around people who vibrate at a higher level than you.

Music has a strong impact on your energy level and vibration, whether you are aware of it or not. Dr. David R. Hawkins's extensive research has shown the music of Bach will make every person go strong, even if they don't personally appreciate classical music. Just as heavy metal music makes everyone go weak, even if it is your favorite sound.

I know from experience that certain music can literally drain me instantly and another song can boost my energy. Not everyone always understood or appreciated my sudden desire to change radio stations or skip forward to another song. I did it because that song was exhausting me. You may or may not be consciously aware of the effect music has on you, but it certainly has a big impact.

Things like music and essential oils are great ways to instantly raise your vibration. The downside is it often works only temporarily. To raise your base vibration and ensure you consistently vibrate at a higher frequency, it's helpful to have a daily practice. Which is why I developed my 21-Day SWEET POWER™ Activations program. These guided activations are created for that specific purpose. Or you can listen to the various free meditations on my Insight Timer profile (the app where you can listen to the audios of this book).

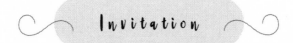

Invitation

Pay more attention to the music you are playing, whether it's at home, in your office, or in your car. Take a moment and pause; feel what that music does to you and your energy level. Does it make you smile, want to sing and dance? Or does it make you tired, does it slow you down? If it's the latter, I suggest you play another song. And use that energy for something more constructive.

The next time you need a little extra energy or inspiration you may want to play some Bach music. As you raise your vibration by doing so, you will have a bigger impact. You have literally increased your reach and ability to create. Even if it's just for a short period of time. Even if you cannot "measure" it yourself. Have fun with it!

\\|/

CHAPTER 21

Seasons and Their Link to Your Energy

Our ancestors consciously worked with the seasons. They planted crops and harvested according to the different phases of the moon. They were much more in sync with the rhythm of nature. Over time, this knowledge and these practices have faded to the background. But it does not lessen our connection to this planet.

The Impact of the Seasons

Some herbs are more potent when gathered during a full moon. Just as jasmine flowers are best picked at night to preserve their scent.

The seasons impact us much more than we think. We forget our body is tied to the natural rhythms of this planet we live on.

> **TRUTH:** At the height of summer when there is much more daylight, we have a lot more energy than in the dead of winter.

No matter how much you wish you were superman or woman, immune to the effects of the seasons, it's a scientific fact that your body has less energy when there is less daylight. Even though the entire world behaves as if that were not true.

In the winter, most of us pretend nothing has changed, and we continue at full speed like it's summer, when our body receives a lot of light and vitamin D. We do not take into account the fact that everyone has less energy in those darker months. As if it does not impact our productivity. We schedule our days pretending we have the same amount of energy on any given day. Our energy levels vary throughout the week and month, but especially throughout the seasons!

I'm baffled that companies do not take this natural rhythm into account when planning projects or even workdays. I believe when we lighten our load as the days shorten, and are in tune with our physical bodies and how much energy we have, we will be more productive, effective, and creative.

The lack of daylight affects our hormones and thus our mood as well. Scandinavia with its extremely short days in winter has one of the highest rates of depressed people, and suicide rates go up everywhere in the autumn. Light therapy was invented for a reason.

I think a world where we pay attention to our physical body and listen to it—not railroad it—is a much happier and healthier world.

Slow Down

I spoke to a dear friend this week and she mentioned she was not as happy—not as enthusiastic—as she normally is. She sought reasons for this in external factors, but I could see it originated from doing too much relative to the amount of energy available to us in winter. [This conversation took place in December.]

If you do not schedule time to relax and recharge you will get grumpy at some point. It's just a matter of time.

When you feel a little less happy, more easily agitated, or plain tired, I recommend you slow down.

> TIP: Ideally, schedule one day a week in which you have no obligations. That allows you to do (and feel!) what your body needs.

We get out of touch with the needs of our body when we keep busy and run on adrenaline. I have done that and adrenaline works well up to the point that it does not. Then you crash.

Now, I don't want you to crash and I guess neither do you, so I urge you to schedule downtime.

December is often the busiest time of the year and you likely have a lot of obligations during that period. Which is exactly why it is extra important to take better care of yourself.

As I mentioned before, your brain needs twenty-four hours to get to a deeper state of relaxation. Your mind needs that deeper relaxation to be able to be fully functional.

Which means not checking emails or thinking about your work for at least one full day and night. For example, no checking emails on Sundays.

It might take some getting used to. I know it did for me. The first Sunday I was not going to check my email, I caught myself plenty of times. Without making a conscious decision to look at my mail, I had already grabbed my phone and pressed the mail icon. The sound of mail coming in was my cue to turn the phone face-down and not read the messages.

What I found fascinating is the number of times I checked my phone without being aware. Chances are you do something similar.

By the way, checking email or social media can literally be addictive because it releases dopamine.

Scary, right?

Rather than get your boost from social media, I urge you to slow down. Plan your days to be a little less full. Go to bed a bit earlier or perhaps sleep in on the weekend. Especially during the winter months. Take that social media and email-free day and you will feel much better. Chances are that seasonal cold will pass you by or at least be over much quicker.

Our Immune System

On the days before and after the spring and autumn equinox, our immune system is at its lowest. As the seasons change, our physical body changes with it. In that period it's paramount to take extra-good care of yourself.

If you feel a cold creeping up or are more tired than usual, it's a sign you need to ease the pressure you are putting on your system. If you continue to overburden yourself, you will pay the price later. I often remind people about this on social media when it gets close to September and March twenty-first. Without exception, people are thrilled to hear it because it explains so much about how unwell they are feeling.

You can diffuse essential oils to boost your immune system. It also helps purify the air by killing bacteria and fungus. Cinnamon bark and clove are especially powerful oils for this purpose. They are wintery spices for a reason.

Drink lots of good quality water so your body can clear out everything it's releasing. Remember to steer clear of water that includes chlorine.

Ground yourself so you are more in touch with your body and will pick up on the first signs of straining yourself.

The Value of Hibernation

Winter calls for an inward focus. Remember, we are tied to nature. In winter, trees slow down their sap flow, slowly growing their roots underground, preparing for spring. That's what we should do, too. Winter is a great time for reflection. To pause and stand still; to contemplate where we are in our life. Get clear on what we appreciate, what is missing. Then act accordingly. Enjoy turning inward. Who knows which powerful insights might surface?

Bears are not the only ones who need a winter sleep. I spoke to a client in early January and she mentioned she needed nine to ten hours of sleep—way more than usual.

I know I need more sleep in the winter, too. Makes total sense given the lack of sunlight and our lower energies. When I give in to the need to sleep more in the winter season, when I honor my connection to the seasons, I get rewarded with more energy.

I know it can be tempting to push through and try to tick things off of your to-do list. It's an illusion that you will get more done like that if you look at the span of a week, let alone a month. Remember, you will not get more done when you skip your lunch break. The same principle applies here.

Taking a walk outside and consciously connecting to nature helps you strengthen the connection to your own physical body, as well.

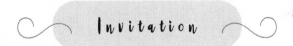

Invitation

Give yourself permission to adjust your schedule and the expected amount of activities according to the seasons. Keep this in mind as you plan your day and week (and year!).

Schedule one email-free day per week (ideally without social media as well) and see how that makes a difference for you. Do not worry if it takes some time to break your habits.

CHAPTER 22

The Curse of Perfectionism

I used to think I had to be perfect to be anything. To be loved, to be appreciated, to be seen, to be valuable. You name it. Not on a conscious level. No, I just had "high standards." And I expected others to live up to those. More importantly, I had to be flawless at everything myself. I worked long hours and I check-check-double-checked everything. I remember my marketing manager saying to me, "Iris, 80% for you is 110% for most people." I was spending a lot of time and energy to get to what felt like 100% to me. With hindsight, I'm guessing not many people would even have noticed the difference. That's obviously not what I thought at the time.

Letting go of the idea that I needed to be perfect has been quite a journey, and I'm still getting better at it. In order to manage and grow your business or career, your relationships and life, you have to let go of perfectionism or you will not get much done. There are always things to be improved and adjusted. If I were to wait until I did everything perfectly, I would not be able to offer much to my clients. Or ever finish this book. And that would serve no one. People are not asking for perfect. They want genuine contact, a true and loving connection, and high-quality experiences.

> **TRUTH**: We think perfection is a failproof
> way to be liked, accepted, and appreciated—
> but denying who we are and what is truly
> important to ourselves is a guaranteed way
> to be exhausted, drained, and miserable.

I thought I was growing by being perfect. That I was being my best by being perfect. Instead, I was limiting myself and slowing down my growth. I was not only hampering the growth of myself and my business, but it was agonizing, frustrating, exhausting, and not at all rewarding. Nowadays I ask myself, *Is it good enough for what I'm trying to accomplish?* I can always come back to it later if I feel I must. Sometimes I do go back and change things, but more often it turns out it's not perfect but pretty good. And certainly good enough!

Do you strive for perfection? It may be in your job or business, in your relationship or your household, in the way you take care of the kids, connect with friends, or how you present yourself. Ask yourself if there is a specific area where you tend to aim for perfect and thus are getting in the way of yourself.

I know from experience that trying to be perfect is a great way to avoid many other things. It's like saying, "please like me and think I am good enough." Remember what I said about wanting to be needed? That is another way of proving to yourself and others that you matter. The solution is deep inside you. Not inside others and what *they* think.

You need to like who you are and learn to love yourself. By taking better care of yourself through managing your energy and becoming aware of what you need and how to set boundaries, you are signaling to yourself that you DO matter and that it's important to take good care of you.

We can be so harsh on ourselves; so much harder than we would ever be on anyone else. In fact, if we witnessed someone treating another person as we sometimes treat ourselves we would probably be shocked and say something about it.

Plus, perfectionism is exhausting; it takes up so much time and energy!

Perfection Paralysis

I wasn't sure I would talk about perfection paralysis. Because it's embarrassing to admit I suffer from it. Perfection paralysis means you would prefer not do something at all rather than risk messing it up. In other words, if you are not certain you are able to do it the way it is supposed to be done (read: to your perfect standards), then instead you avoid doing it altogether. Because hey, at least you didn't ruin it!

For me, this plays out with laundry. I happily blame my mother for that. She's the laundry guru. In fact, she's a walking Wikipedia when it comes to pretty much anything, not just household stuff. She's the queen of removing stains. When your former boyfriend calls to ask if you have tips on how to remove the stain from his favorite shirt (some of my mom's laundry skills rubbed off on me), you know what time it is.

Back to my laundry. I have a few permanent residents at the bottom of my hamper. A flimsy silk nightgown I bought in Italy and the anti-fly net from my visit to Uluru, Australia. I don't want to wash them to shreds. Instead I don't wash them at all. I'm laughing out loud as I type this, because of course it's ridiculous.

[Update: I recently moved and my mom found these poor ones at the bottom of my laundry bag. Mom rescued them and offered to take them with her to wash. Yay! Problem solved. For now.]

Anyway, I decided to share this in case you have perfection paralysis in some area of your life. I know, chances are slim. Likely it's not about your delicate laundry, either. But on the off-chance you recognize the tendency, consider this your nudge to perhaps outsource the problem.

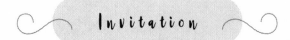

Invitation

In which areas of your life do you tend to want to do things perfectly? Is it in your job, your relationships, the way you do things in the house? What comes to mind first? Then start there. See where you are holding yourself to ridiculous standards, where you can start doing things a little less perfectly—and you will get a lot of time and energy in return.

CHAPTER 23

Working from Home

We are in the middle of a pandemic as I write this. The world looks different than normal. In crazy times, I know one of the first things that goes out the window is self-care. Because you simply do not have the time. Or you are too busy being stressed or worried. Perhaps you are grieving.

These are all understandable reasons why self-care might not be a priority. I believe it should be. Even when you barely have time to take a shower, when your business or livelihood is at stake, or you have lost a loved one. Especially then!

Self-care is not a luxury. It's not something you do when you have ticked off all your other boxes and when your to-do list has dwindled to an agreeable level. It's not for the fainthearted or the ones who take it easy. Self-care is a serious commitment.

Have you ever seen a professional athlete go "easy" on their self-care? Likely not—or not with success. Their success is based on them focusing on what they need to excel.

I have worked closely with elite athletes. I know what their schedule looks like and how strict they need to be when it comes to not only food and exercise, but rest as well.

If you want to be successful at your job or business, in fact if you want to be successful at life—you need to take your self-care extremely seriously.

Knowing what you and your body need and being able to give it to yourself is the foundation for everything.

Blurring the Lines

A lot of people get tired of working from home. Not just mentally, but physically and emotionally as well.

A few weeks ago, I facilitated a brainstorming training session and the participants felt like they were invited to a party. They got to go to the office! Most of them had not been there for six months. It was fun to witness their excitement, but I was confronted by how much they had missed live interaction with colleagues.

It's important to find new ways to take care of yourself and to establish healthy boundaries while you work from home.

Where before there were natural borders between home and work, now things get very much blurred. Especially if you do not have the luxury of a dedicated office space in your house.

I have been working from my home office for the past nineteen years, so I have had plenty of time to practice.

Here are my top three tips to make working from home a little easier on the senses:

1. **Make as much of a distinction between work and time off as you can.** Preferably work from a different room or at least a different corner of the living room. If that's not feasible then try to put your work away at night so it's not visible. Throw a scarf over your laptop if you have to—anything to stop seeing your work. If you must work from your bedroom, make sure to air it after you are done working.

2. **Try to have specific "work" and "private" times.** Ideally, work during the day and relax at night. That rhythm will also do wonders for your sleep. You should not be in front of a screen

for at least the last hour before you go to bed. The blue light lowers the production of melatonin, the hormone that helps you fall asleep.

3. **Wearing different clothes helps, too.** Keep your business suit or smart clothes for work, and change into something more comfortable once you are done. Much like you might have done when you went into the office.

All these steps signal to your brain that you are switching from work mode to time off. In the past, your trip home served as a ritual to shift focus from work to your private life. When you take away the travel time, you need something else to serve as that signal.

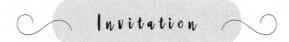

Invitation

Which of these tips speak to you? Since there is no time like the present, I recommend you start implementing the tips you resonate with straight away.

Self-Care Behind Your Screen

These days most people spend more time behind a computer screen than ever before. Here are a few quick tips and mini breaks you can use to make sure you do not deplete yourself and overburden your physical body. Some of these pointers are probably obvious, but I know we do not always implement everything we are aware of. If you are already doing this, great!

Blink! When we stare at a screen we do not blink as much as when we speak to people in person. This means your eyes will dry out and get irritated.

Get up and move at least once per hour. Set a timer if you have to remind yourself. Rotate your shoulders, stretch your arms and legs. Take a few deep breaths.

Drink plenty of water. When we watch TV or look at screens our brains literally use more water. Be sure to hydrate yourself and you might stave off a headache at an early stage and keep productivity high.

Make sure your workspace supports you. Check that your chair and desk are the right height for your build. Elevate your screen so you can look straight ahead. No need to put extra strain on your neck and shoulders. I use a stack of inspiring books to raise my laptop and I type on a separate keyboard. Much more ergonomic.

Be aware of your posture. I know I have a tendency to lean forward, as if it will make things go faster. I consciously need to remind myself to lean back and place both feet firmly on the floor.

Open windows. Unless it will make you freeze or feel too hot, open your windows to air your office space daily. Our brain needs oxygen to function fully and the more fresh air, the more productive you will be.

Ground yourself daily.

Take breaks. Remember that your brain needs a regular pause in order to be most productive. Aside from stepping away from your computer for lunch, getting outside for some fresh air is hopefully an obvious choice to recharge body and mind.

For shorter breaks, I created this three-minute Mini-Meditation. A quick way to relax and recharge so you will be fresh again for your next meeting or work sprint. Listen to my Get Centered – Mini-Meditation at **www.radianttools.nl**.

CHAPTER 24

The Power of Gratitude

What you focus on, you attract. That's what you are feeding—literally. It's how your brain works.

Like when you are skiing or driving and you spot a big tree and you want to be sure to steer clear of it. But you keep looking at the tree. Guess where you will end up?

Exactly. Smash in the middle of the tree.

That's how it works with everything you concentrate on. Your brain will go, *Oh is that what you want? We can arrange that.* It will find all kinds of ways to steer you to whatever image you hold in your mind.

Your brain does not distinguish between whether you do or do not want the thing you are focusing on. It only follows orders and aims for whatever you feed it with.

Did you know your brain makes no distinction between whether something is actually happening or whether you are dreaming it up, either? Athletes use that power to visualize the perfect race. What is so cool is that by simply visualizing a certain physical exercise your muscles actually get stronger!

Remember: your brain focuses on nightmares and daydreams alike! Hence the key is to feed your brain with only those things you want to happen or create. I know that is not always easy, especially when things are not going your way, or you are busy or even ill.

Here's where the power of gratitude comes into play. This tool is as easy as it is powerful. Gratitude is a unique instrument to shift your focus from negative to positive, from worry and concern to appreciation.

Remember all those times you thought, "I'll feel better when…" whether that was being in a relationship, improving your health or finances, or having less stress at work.

Now, what if you did not need to change any of your circumstances to feel better? You can! I have witnessed these changes firsthand with my individual clients and with the participants of the four Gratitude Projects I have hosted. For a period of thirty-three days, participants received daily tips and inspiration, allowing them to consciously focus on gratitude and share five things they are grateful for that day on our private forum. It was extremely powerful to see the shift participants made over the course of a few weeks, no matter where they lived in the world.

Even when their outer circumstances stayed the same, participants felt much better about their lives. Their attitude had shifted to be more positive and they were able to identify a lot of things they were thankful for. Even in difficult circumstances, like moving homes, divorce, or the terminal illness of a loved one.

This is what one participant shared:

"I did my first Gratitude Project several years ago during a time when I thought my world was falling apart. I quickly came to appreciate how a gratitude practice helped to reframe the experience and to increase my resilience when facing new challenges. I hesitated to join this time due to other things on my plate, but a friend—who I "met" through my first Gratitude Project and who has kept in touch— wisely reminded me that I should join precisely because of the other

things on my plate! The changes I have seen in myself since doing my first Gratitude Project really speak to our ability to change and rewire our brains in positive ways!"

Gratitude is heavily researched and its power is well documented. Gratitude leads to less stress and feeling calmer. It greatly increases happiness and even impacts your physical health in ways such as longer and better-quality sleep. I believe it boosts your immune system and reduces all kinds of health risks. Pretty powerful stuff. But even if you would never notice the physical benefits, it's extremely valuable to have a tool to help you focus on what you want more of, rather than worry about all the things you do not want.

> **TRUTH:** Gratitude is a shortcut to happiness, feeling calmer, and reducing stress. You will experience more ease and joy in your life. It also helps raise your vibration and release lower-level energies such as fear and "not enough."

When you embrace an attitude of gratitude, you will benefit from that for the rest of your life. I believe all the tools in this book will help you make a positive shift, but this is one of my favorite.

Being grateful is a matter of looking at the things in your life that you appreciate. If you can turn your attention to being grateful for what you *do* have—because we all have something to be grateful for—you open the doors wide to more good things coming into your life.

The power comes in when you are able to *feel* the gratitude; when you are able to connect with that emotion. The more explicit you are, the better it works. Rather than thinking, *I'm grateful for today's sun*, try being more specific. *I'm grateful for the warmth of the sun on my face when I walked in the park and paused to take it in.* The latter makes it easier to bring yourself back to that moment and connect with how it felt to stand in the sunshine.

On a happy day, it will be easy to find things to be grateful for. But I promise you that even on difficult days, there is something to be thankful for. You will have to search a little harder for it, I grant you that, but it's always there. In times of crisis you simply have to dig a little deeper to find things you can appreciate. Making the effort on tough days is what strengthens your gratitude muscle the most. Do not give up too easily. On any given day you must be able to find at least three things you can be thankful for. No matter how small it is. It could be the food in your fridge, the fact you did not get rained upon, or that you spoke to a friend. The event does not have to be grand. There is powerful gratitude in the small things, too.

Gratitude is one of the quickest ways to shift your focus and energy. You can only feel one emotion at a time, so when you feel grateful, you cannot be worried or angry or sad. Give it a try! It really works wonders.

Future Gratitudes

It's important to remember your desires are first fulfilled in consciousness and then will become tangible.

In other words: your wishes and dreams will first manifest energetically before they will become visible. That principle inspired me to think about gratitude in advance. It's fun to think about things that have not yet happened and be grateful for them *as if* they have already come to pass.

Use the powerful tool of your imagination and the knowledge that we create with our thoughts and our energy to attract new things into our life. It's what I like to call "Future Gratitudes."

TIP: State your Future Gratitudes pretending they have already happened. Start by saying "I *am* grateful for..." I often hear people make the mistake of saying, "I *will* be grateful for..." Saying "I will" pushes it away from you, while "I am" pulls it closer. Can you sense the difference?

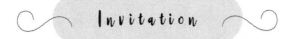

Invitation

Gratitude is one of the most transformational tools to have in your kit, and I suggest you start using it straight away. At the beginning or end of your day, take a few minutes to reflect and think of at least three things (ideally five) you are grateful for, and write them down. Anchoring this new practice to a specific moment during your day—like with the grounding—makes it easier to embed this new habit. Some people like to do it in bed to start or end their day with gratitude. Others begin with gratitude at their desk. Find a moment that works for you.

Once you are clear on the first thing you are thankful for, take a moment and allow yourself to *feel* that gratitude. Don't make it something you check off of your to-do list. The power lies in feeling grateful. Get in touch with that feeling and take in the appreciation for a few breaths.

I recommend you play with Future Gratitudes as well. It's a lot of fun and quite powerful.

You can listen to the Start Your Day With Gratitude meditation at **www.radianttools.nl** if you want me to talk you through your gratitude practice.

You'll notice gratitude is contagious. The more you do it, the more you want to do it. I often hear participants start to share the things they are grateful for with their loved ones or colleagues. I like to see it as a beautiful catalyst for positivity, rolling around the globe like a snowball filled with happiness, ever-increasing in volume and velocity.

Bonus: express your gratitude. Sharing what you are thankful for with the people you care for is like handing out invisible packages of love and appreciation. Especially when you thank someone for something they did, for being who they are, or sharing what they mean to you!

Looking Forward

We've covered a lot of ground together and the amount of insights and information might feel a little overwhelming. I hope this book has given you more clarity on the things you can do to have more energy, live a life you love, and shine. It's not about changing who you are, but about understanding how certain activities, emotions, and people impact you and how you can design your day, actions, and surroundings so they support you, rather than drain you. Letting go of "shoulds" and adding more actions that light you up is a great way to become more radiant.

Here's a quick overview of what I recommend you start with:

1. Ingrain the three steps: ground; cleanse your energy field; protect your energy.

2. Remember the 20% rule: stop before you're tired so you can support your physical body in recharging fully.

3. Implement insights from your Daily Energy Inventory. Know what increases your energy and what depletes it—this information will help you plan better!

4. Using that information, plan your day and week so your schedule supports your personal rhythm. Take baby steps where you can. This doesn't have to happen overnight!

5. Include me-time, one hour minimum per day.
6. Remember the twenty-four-hour wind-down period; take at least one day OFF per week.
7. Start setting the most urgent healthy boundaries and communicate those boundaries with the people involved.
8. Be aware of your emotions and how they impact you.
9. Focus on consciously raising your vibration.
10. Practice gratitude daily.

If you begin implementing these practices, then you have already taken a huge step forward to reclaiming your energy.

Once you feel like you can take on more, I suggest rereading the chapters that spoke to you most and starting to implement the tips and invitations from that topic.

If you would prefer more support in this process, my SWEET POWER™ "Energy Management for Sensitive Souls" program might be a good fit.

If you know you would do better with more accountability and highly personal support, consider private mentoring with me.

And if you are interested in bringing this topic into your organization, then check out www.radiantemployees.com.

The Impact of Change

Your personal change often impacts your relationships with other people. Usually for the better. However, on a few occasions people can feel threatened by your shift. They are afraid to lose the person they knew, or worry *they* now have to change.

One friend of mine felt anxious when I told her about my intuitive abilities. She was afraid to let go of the Iris she knew. Most of my friends were thrilled and excited for me when I explained my discovery that I could tune in for people and sense what is off or what they need to return to balance. They appreciated I had taken the time to describe my process and allowed them to be a part of my journey. Some were inspired by the shifts I made. Others were curious.

The solution is not to avoid change. That's not what I was trying to accomplish. Change is imperative. Stagnant water becomes stale—nothing healthy will grow there.

No matter how people respond, keep in mind that you are doing what needs to be done for you to have more energy and be happier. To be able to love your life. I believe when you do what is truly right for you, everyone will benefit in the long run.

Expect some inner resistance as well. Resistance is an indication that you are stepping out of your comfort zone and entering uncharted territory. Which is a great sign because you want things to change. You want more energy, clearer boundaries, etc. Do not step back even when you feel the resistance. Take some time to look at the source of your resistance. Tell this part of you, "I choose this." Embrace the change and move forward with conviction, knowing you are taking the right steps by taking better care of yourself and, in turn, those around you.

Trust and believe in yourself. You are reading this for a reason. You already took that next step when you picked up this book. Trust yourself, trust the process, and trust you will be guided and provided with the insights, information, support, and encouragement when and where you need it. If it is hard to find or feel, reach out and ask for support. There is no need to do this alone or to suffer.

Giving you a big hug.

Enjoy the journey!

Much love,

Iris

My Gratitude

Honestly, it felt a little like cheating—allowing myself to create this book before completing the sequel of my novel *Poisoned Arrow*. But I'm so glad I did! Writing this book was an interesting process of looking back at several formative moments in my life. I loved how the red thread of moving from willpower to SWEET POWER™ allowed me to see things in a new perspective. Hindsight made abundantly clear these shifts were only able to occur thanks to a combination of my desire to grow and the need to change—given specific circumstances. My personal search for a way to feel better about being me and enjoying life, without being drained by people and the demands of living, resulted in the tools and tips described in this book.

I am grateful for everyone who has played the role of catalyst in some shape or form. Allowing me to make a shift, urging me to set clearer boundaries, nudging me to take better care of myself.

Huge gratitude to my parents for providing a safe space to learn and grow, and for stimulating continuous education.

Big hug to my brother Paul—even though we're very different I'm so grateful to have you in my life!

Many people played an important role on my journey. I would like to highlight some key players here. Brigitte, our almost daily conversations keep me sane, and provide plenty of reasons for laughing out loud. Elles, I'm so grateful you were the first to accept me for who I am—quirks included. Inge, thank you for being there when I needed you most. Monique, ever since Management Essentials it's been a joy to be connected.

Huge thanks to my clients! I am grateful for your trust. It's a pleasure to support you in embracing your SWEET POWER™ and I'm honored to be a part of your journey.

I'm thankful for my amazing editor, Allison. Your emails always light a fire in me to make changes or rearrange copy, and to become a better writer. I couldn't have done this without you.

Thank you, Domini, for another incredible design. I love the cover, once I got past the idea of putting my picture on it ;), and the interior is simply beautiful.

I would like to thank my beta readers: Henk, Jessica, Mariëlle, Mark, Paul and Susan. I so appreciate your thoughtful feedback and ideas. Your comments have been invaluable in strengthening the book.

Lots of thanks to my proofreaders David, Jan, and Tracy for crossing t's and dotting i's!

Last but certainly not least, thank *you*, dear reader, for trusting me with your time. I hope this book has given you valuable tools and new ideas on how to take better care of yourself, have more energy and—most importantly—love your life more!

Reference List

Aaron, Elaine N. *Hoog Sensitieve Personen.* Translated by Marja Waterman. Amsterdam: Uitgeverij Archipel, 2004.

Hawkins, David R, M.D., Ph.D. *Power vs. Force. The Hidden Determinants of Human Behavior.* Hay House, 2004.

Kelly, Jack. "Indeed Study Shows That Worker Burnout Is At Frighteningly High Levels: Here Is What You Need To Do Now." *Forbes.* April 5, 2021. https://www.forbes.com/sites/jackkelly/2021/04/05/indeed-study-shows-that-worker-burnout-is-at-frighteningly-high-levels-here-is-what-you-need-to-do-now/?sh=43fa150223bb

Laub, Marcy. "Skin deep." *Sustainability at Harvard.* Harvard University, September 23, 2015. https://green.harvard.edu/news/skin-deep

Moritz, Andreas. *The Key to Health and Rejuvenation: Breakthrough Medicine For The 21ˢᵗ Century.* USA: 1ˢᵗ Books Library, 1998.

Moritz, Andreas. *Timeless Secrets of Health & Rejuvenation: Breakthrough Medicine For the 21ˢᵗ Century.* USA: Lightning Source, 2009.

Roeder, Amy. "Harmful, untested chemicals rife in personal care products." *School of Public Health at Harvard.* Harvard University, February 13, 2014. https://www.hsph.harvard.edu/news/features/harmful-chemicals-in-personal-care-products/

Rosenblatt, Carolyn. "Magic Touch: Six Things You Can Do to Connect in a Disconnected World." *Forbes.* January 8, 2011. https://www.forbes.com/sites/carolynrosenblatt/2011/01/18/magic-touch-six-things-you-can-do-to-connect-in-a-disconnected-world

Van Dam, Nick and Van der Helm, Els. "There's a Proven Link Between Effective Leadership and Getting Enough Sleep." *Harvard Business Review.* February 16, 2016. https://hbr.org/2016/02/theres-a-proven-link-between-effective-leadership-and-getting-enough-sleep

Weisgerber, Ryan M. "Power vs. Force by David R. Hawkins: Part 2." *Hug the Universe.* https://www.hugtheuniverse.com/blog/how-to-identify-truth-in-a-confusing-world (Accessed January 18, 2022)

About the Author

Iris van Ooyen is the creator of the SWEET POWER™ approach to personal and career development, growth, and self-care designed for those who have big things to do in this world, but who often feel drained by the demand that showing up big requires.

Through her research, she's identified *four distinctive stages* that sensitive souls experience in their growth process, and the core of her work lies in helping that particular audience determine where they are on the growth curve, and discover the right steps to move forward—*and* shine bright.

Iris is a firm believer in combining the inner and the outer, the spiritual and the practical.

Thanks to her intuitive abilities, she can go straight to the core of what is preventing you from being your healthy, radiant self, and by immediately applying healing energy you will make deep and lasting shifts on layers you can't get to on your own.

An MBA with a background in corporate marketing, Iris combines her extensive business experience with her renowned razor-sharp intuitive insights in order to support those struggling in their career, business, or life and high performance as a whole. Her clients—including Olympic athletes, entrepreneurs, business managers and teams—praise her ability to quickly zero in on what is not working and facilitate energetic transformations that carry over into all aspects of life and work.

www.radiantbook.nl

If you would like more support in this process, Iris's SWEET POWER™ "Energy Management for Sensitive Souls" program is a great next step. Read all about this online program at:

www.energymanagementsystem.nl